CANADIANS WITH CUSTER

CANADIANS ❧ WITH ❧ CUSTER

MARY THOMAS

DUNDURN
TORONTO

Editor: Jennifer McKnight
Design: Jesse Hooper
Printer: Webcom

Library and Archives Canada Cataloguing in Publication

Thomas, Mary
          Canadians with Custer / by Mary Thomas.

Includes bibliographical references.
Also issued in electronic format.
ISBN 978-1-4597-0407-7

          1. Little Bighorn, Battle of the, Mont., 1876--Participation, Canadian. I. Title.

E83.876.T55 2012   973.8'2   C2012-900097-3

1   2   3   4   5   16   15   14   13   12

We acknowledge the support of the **Canada Council for the Arts** and the **Ontario Arts Council** for our publishing program. We also acknowledge the financial support of the **Government of Canada** through the **Canada Book Fund** and **Livres Canada Books**, and the **Government of Ontario** through the **Ontario Book Publishing Tax Credit** and the **Ontario Media Development Corporation**.

Care has been taken to trace the ownership of copyright material used in this book. The author and the publisher welcome any information enabling them to rectify any references or credits in subsequent editions.

J. Kirk Howard, President

Printed and bound in Canada.
www.dundurn.com

Dundurn
3 Church Street, Suite 500
Toronto, Ontario, Canada
M5E 1M2

Gazelle Book Services Limited
White Cross Mills
High Town, Lancaster, England
LA1 4XS

Dundurn
2250 Military Road
Tonawanda, NY
U.S.A. 14150

For Pat,
Mark, Sean, and Mikhail

TABLE OF CONTENTS

ACKNOWLEDGEMENTS

A N AUTHOR OF HISTORICAL WORK OFTEN PEERS OVER THE shoulders of librarians, archivists, historians, and history buffs to gain an insight into the subject, leans on them to obtain help in searching for information. I want to acknowledge a number of people who allowed me to do just that. They passed along their knowledge freely and with good will.

Diane Merkel of the Little Bighorn History Alliance and members of the Alliance were instrumental in throwing me into all things Custer — good or bad. Marie Wright of Belleville Public Library helped with my research requests, no matter how arcane.

Dave Schafer, Washita Battlefield National Historic Site, Cheyenne, Oklahoma, and Bonnie Whitecloud of the Manataka American Indian Council, Hot Springs, Arizona, were important sources regarding aboriginal history of the southern plains. I want to thank Diana Everett of the Oklahoma Historical Society for permission to use information from her history of Chief Black Kettle.

Karl Katafiasz and Charmaine Wawrzyniec, Monroe County Library, Ellis Reference and Information Centre, Monroe, Michigan, were ever helpful with Custer references. Others who provided help along the way include: Zoe Ann Stoltz, Historical Society of Montana; Margaret Houghton, Hamilton Public Library; Jamie Serran, Yarmouth County Museum and Archives, Yarmouth, Nova Scotia; Bill Stevens, St. Catharines Historical Society; Mike O'Byrne, Heritage Mount Pleasant; Ralph Laviolette, Huron County Historical Society (Walton); Dakota Goodhouse and Al Johnson,

Fort Abraham Lincoln Foundation, North Dakota; John Doerner and Jerry Jasmer, National Park Service, Little Bighorn Battlefield National Monument; Ron Pickard, Little Big Horn Associates; author Steve Arnold; and the many who helped with the photo hunt.

And, as always, a thank you to my reader, Emily Stassen Cramer.

PROLOGUE

IN THE HISTORY OF THE NORTH AMERICAN WEST, THE STORY
of Custer's Last Stand — Lieutenant-Colonel, Brevet Major-
General, George A. Custer's battle at Little Big Horn in 1876 — is
a familiar one. The massacre of Custer and his troops is indicative of
the way the United States won the west, except that Custer's defeat is
an unusual victory for the Plains Indians. What is less known is the
story of the seventeen Canadians who were with the Seventh Cavalry,
and/or at Little Big Horn on that fateful day.

The settling of the North American west is a story of expansion
pushed by immigration: need for land, greed for land. While this was,
with a few exceptions, an evolution pushed by commerce in Canada,
the same cannot be said for the United States, where "Indian Wars"
were the common method of expansion. But both sides of the border
held the same concept: the Native peoples were pushed from their
traditional lands into pockets, or reservations, that held them in a
precarious peace.

In the United States the Native tribes were displaced by the
influx of immigrants. This migration west in the 1800s was supported and advanced by a series of armed forts, with army patrols
putting pressure on the Indian population. There was apprehension
on both sides; the settlers fearing Indian raids, the Natives fearing
loss of territory and their way of life.

In 1829, President Andrew Jackson, called Sharp Knife by
the Indians, gave his first address to congress, recommending
that the Indians be removed westward beyond the Mississippi. "I

suggest the propriety of setting apart an ample district west of the Mississippi ... to be guaranteed to the Indian tribes, as long as they shall occupy it."[1]

When the war with Mexico ended in 1847, the United States took possession of a vast expanse of territory reaching from Texas to California. All of it was west of the (supposedly) "permanent Indian frontier."[2]

The great chiefs of the Plains Indians signed treaties with the United States government, only to see those treaties broken over and over again by the U.S. Army on behalf of the government. Indian agents cheated them; soldiers massacred them. The aboriginals were victims of cruel, systemic injustices, and corrupt administrators.

The pressure for land intensified following the end of the Civil War in the mid-1860s. The army moved to Kansas, then farther west. Lieutenant-Colonel Custer, who had earned fame and celebrity during the Civil War, was now sent into Indian Territory as head of the Seventh Cavalry. Some people hate him, some love him: "Custerophobes and Custerophiles." While Custer certainly proved himself militarily in the Civil War, many resented his perceived arrogance and love of celebrity. I've tried to stay somewhat objective, although the arrogance and celebrity are hard to ignore.

The tradition at that time, in the United States Army, of a person having and using both regular army and volunteer rank designations can be confusing. I find it often depends on whether the author was in favour, or not in favour, of the person being cited. If in favour, the author of the manuscript or letter tended to use the more elaborate, or higher, volunteer rank. I have tried to stick to the army ranks; maybe not always successfully.

Tens of thousands of Canadians, British North Americans at the time, fought in the Civil War. They were there for the adventure, or the generous signing bonuses being offered. Some were kidnapped by squads of "recruiters" from armies of both the north and south who crossed the border to get men or young boys to boost their ranks.

Some Canadians who followed Custer to Little Big Horn in Montana in 1876 had already been in the Civil War, and continued on as "soldiers of fortune" or as a natural continuation of their army service as a job. Some of them were close friends, or at least admirers, of Custer. Others were mercenaries wanting a job with adventure.

This book is their story.

CHAPTER 1

THE SEVENTH CAVALRY, JUNE 1867

T HE CANADIAN, LIEUTENANT WILLIAM WINER COOKE, WAS in command of the wagon train. Along with Lieutenant Samuel M. Robbins and Company D, he was heading back to camp from Fort Wallace, Kansas territory. Patrols were on the alert for Indians. Since the twelve wagons were full of supplies, the going was slower than it had been on the way out. It was guide Will Comstock who spotted them through his field glasses, on a level plateau, on the horizon.

The Indians boldly rode the crest; a few dozen, then a hundred appeared, all of them in full war dress — war bonnets, war paint, buffalo-hide shields. Most of them were armed with carbines and revolvers, some with bows and arrows as well. Some reports say the numbers reached as many as six hundred. Company D numbered fifty troops.

Lieutenant Cooke ordered the wagon train into two parallel columns, wide enough to let the cavalry ride between them. With only fifty soldiers — forty-eight men and two officers — defence was the only option. The men dismounted to form a circle around the wagon train; some of them detailed to hold the horses between the wagon lines. Lieutenant Cooke ordered the wagon masters to keep the wagons moving, and close together.

The Indians made the first attack on one flank. The troopers waited until they were within short range. Dropping to one knee, they poured a volley into the attackers. The Indians retreated. Comstock led the cheers. He concluded:

There is no sich good luck for us to think them injuns mean to give it up so. Six hundreds reds devils ain't agoin' to let fifty men stop them from gettin' at the sugar and coffee that is in these wagons. And they ain't agoin' to be satisfied until they get some of our scalps to pay for the bucks we popped out of their saddles a bit ago.[1]

The game resumed. This time the Indians used their trick of "circling." The chiefs led off, followed by the warriors in single file until hundreds of warriors formed a huge circle enclosing the wagons and the fifty troopers. The Indians rode their ponies at top speed, all the time issuing war whoops. They closed the circle little by little as the wagon train continued its slow progress. The warriors threw themselves to the far side of the ponies, each exposing only a head and a single foot, aiming their guns over or under the ponies' necks.

The troopers opened fire. The running battle lasted nearly three hours. The cavalry ammunition was running low. The only possible relief was nightfall or reinforcements. Luck was with them. The attackers spotted a dark line on the horizon that seemed to be moving. Sending a final volley of bullets and arrows into the wagon train, the Indians disappeared over the bluffs.

Expecting only a short respite and not aware of the thin dark line on the horizon, the men dealt with the wounded troopers over the next hour. Then they spotted unidentified horsemen approaching. Through field glasses they could see it was blue-shirted cavalry. Lieutenant Cooke and Bill Comstock and a few troopers rushed out to meet them. It was Captain Robert M. West, who, with Company K, had travelled with Cooke's wagon train on its way out to Fort Wallace, but left it midway at Beaver Creek. He and his men had orders to scout up and down the creek area for Indians, then await Cooke's return journey.

Meanwhile, back at the Seventh Cavalry camp on the Republican River in west Kansas, seventy miles from Fort Wallace,

Lieutenant-Colonel George Armstrong Custer had been getting worried. Custer had won acclaim as a soldier of the army of the north during the recent United States Civil War. He was young, just twenty-eight; this was his first real foray into Indian country, and he was in command of this operation.

Custer had just learned that another mission, headed by Major Joel Elliott in the other direction, had encountered no Indians. This, he was sure, meant the war parties would be looking out for the wagon train loaded with supplies. Custer sent a squadron of men out to Beaver Creek to join Captain West. He told them to head toward Fort Wallace until they met the wagon train, and escort it back. The troopers marched to Beaver Creek non-stop, and the combined forces arrived just in time to save Cooke's wagon convoy.

There had been ongoing concerns about cholera, and Custer was worried about his wife, who was at Fort Hays. He had expected her to travel to Fort Wallace, and so he sent a letter that Cooke carried with him, instructing Libbie Custer to travel back to camp under Cooke's personal protection. Finding she was not there, Cooke rode on to Fort Hays, but General Hancock would not give her permission to leave, fearing a possible Indian attack on the wagons. Most officers of the regiment knew what that meant, and Cooke explained it to Libbie Custer:

> The tall slender Canadian explained that Custer had given all his officers instructions, should ever Mrs. Custer be under their escort when attacked by Indians, it was their duty to kill her immediately, taking no chances that she would fall into the hands of the Indians.[2]

Another occurrence added to the concerns. Newly appointed Second Lieutenant Lyman S. Kidder, twenty-five years old and with an escort of ten men, many even younger, was ordered to carry important dispatches from General W.T. Sherman to Custer. All the young men were inexperienced in Indian warfare; they were on a suicide mission, really. Not hearing from Kidder, Custer then followed his original orders to head across the country from the Platte River to Smoky Hill River at Fort Wallace.

It was near the end of June 1867. After Cooke's contingent with the supply wagons caught up with the rest, Custer and the Seventh Cavalry continued on the circle as proposed by General Philip Sheridan, keeping alert for hostile Indians. This route was close to the overland route of travel westward to the newly discovered mine claims in Colorado Territory. The combination of danger from Indian attack and the allure of mining for gold or silver so close by was too much for some of the troopers. In one day on the Platte River, thirty-five men deserted, out of a force of less than three hundred on the march. The deserters left early on the morning of July 7, 1867. Custer had no chance of recovering them, so his cavalry headed out at five in the morning as planned, travelling southward across a prairie of cacti.

After fifteen miles he called a rest stop. About a third of the troopers, thinking they were camped for the rest of the day, planned to desert that night into the mountains. When the order was given to repack and resume the march, thirteen of the soldiers, seven on horseback, left camp heading north as fast as they could. They ignored shouts from the officers and the bugle "recall." Desertion in broad daylight. Officers of the guard were ordered to the chase.

Major Elliott, Lieutenant Cooke, and seven troopers hit a gallop. The deserting horsemen couldn't be overtaken, but Major Elliott ordered those on foot to halt. There were varying reports on how the scene played out from there. Some reports indicate one of the deserters raised his carbine to fire at the pursuers and Elliott's group opened fire. Others say the deserters laid down their arms, then the officers fired on them. Three of the deserters were hit and wounded in the first volley, one later died; the remaining three surrendered.

The quick action against the deserters cut short any plan of escape during that night; there were no more desertions for the remainder of the campaign. But it precipitated a court martial against Custer two months later.

Custer's cavalry kept going, and just two days out of Fort Wallace, Comstock spotted signs on the trail. Custer later described the scene:

> Hastening, in common with many others of the party, to his side, a sight met our gaze which even at this remote day makes my very blood curdle. Lying in irregular order, and within a very limited circle, were the mangled bodies of poor Kidder and his party, yet so brutally hacked and disfigured as to be beyond recognition save as human beings.[3]

Custer and his column reached camp at Fort Wallace on July 13, having completed 705 miles on the trail. Fort Wallace was the last and most western military outpost in Kansas; it could accommodate about 500 men. Troopers were moved out from there to guard various stations of the Smoky Hill stage route, to escort the stage coaches and wagon trains, or protect railway construction crews. For the past two months it had endured repeated Indian raids. The man in charge was Captain Myles W. Keogh, commander of the post as well as Company I of the Seventh U.S. Cavalry.

Nearby was the Pond Creek Station, a fortified stopping place for the stage coaches. On June 26, a band of 300 Cheyennes, led by Chief Roman Nose, had attacked the Pond Creek Station, making off with horses of the overland Stage Company. Heading for Fort Wallace, they were met by Captain Albert Barnitz and the full Company G of the Seventh Cavalry. The cavalry lost seven troopers, some of them mutilated, and had to retreat to the fort.

While his troopers set up camp, Custer checked in at Fort Wallace to find it virtually under siege. Travel along the Smoky Hill trail had ground to a halt because of Indian activity. No mail or dispatches were getting through. And more than that, cholera was spreading, with deaths occurring almost daily. Food was running low, and the end of the railway was 200 miles away, the supply depot farther still.

There was no word from his commander General Winfield S. Hancock, but Lieutenant-Colonel Custer decided to chance it. He chose about seventy-five of his men to break the siege. They left the fort at sunset on July 15, 1867. He followed the Smoky Hill stage route east, expecting to cover the 150 miles to Fort Hays, Kansas, as quickly as possible. His plan was to continue to Fort Harker with half a dozen men, while Captain Lewis Hamilton followed with the rest of the command. Custer would have the wagon train loaded for the return trip.

There were twelve stage stations between Fort Wallace and Fort Hays, about ten miles apart. Custer's command marched at night, travelling from station to station. This was tricky since the station staff was on the lookout for the enemy and would fire at the sound of a voice, even an English one. They reached Fort Hays at three in the morning of July 18 — they had travelled 150 miles in fifty-five hours, including rest stops.

Still with no orders, Custer and two of his favourites, his younger brother Lieutenant Tom Custer and the Canadian Lieutenant William Winer Cooke, plus two troopers, immediately struck out for Fort Harker. They reached it at two in the morning on July 19. Custer sent out telegrams to headquarters and Fort Sedgwick telling of the fate of Kidder's party, and made arrangements for the arrival of Captain Hamilton and loading of the supply train.

This was when Custer made a decision that changed the course of his life. With the worry about the cholera, and rationalizing that he had time on his hands, he decided to make a family visit. He hadn't made contact through the mails at Fort Wallace with Mrs. Custer. And the conditions at the fort when he was there were appalling — troopers succumbing to cholera or being killed by Indians, the food was bad, and supplies for the horses were low. Custer felt the lack of supplies had prevented him from waging an all-out campaign in the Indian wars. But most telling, he had left Fort Wallace without direct orders from General Hancock.

Now, after reporting to his superior officer at Fort Harker, Colonel Andrew J. Smith, Custer felt that he had no immediate responsibilities until the wagon train was ready: "I applied for and received authority to visit Fort Riley, about ninety miles east of Harker by rail, where my family was then located."

Just hours after his arrival at Fort Harker, on the morning of July 19, he took the train to Fort Riley to visit his wife. Almost immediately he received a telegram from Colonel Smith ordering him to return to his command.

The train service was erratic. Custer and his wife, Libbie, didn't get a train until the 21st. As soon as he reported to Smith he was arrested. General Hancock had ordered Colonel Smith to lay the charges.[4]

Seeing that Mrs. Custer had arrived as well, Smith ordered Custer back to Fort Riley to remain under arrest and to await his court martial. The charge: leaving his command at Fort Wallace without authority.

In the meantime, Captain Hamilton had arrived at Fort Harker. He, along with Lieutenants William Cooke and Tom Custer, returned with the loaded supply wagon to Fort Wallace. Major Elliott assumed command of the Seventh Cavalry while Custer was under arrest.

There were various motives involved in the charges against Custer. They were pressed by General Hancock, although they had been laid by Smith. Hancock was getting criticism from Washington that his summer Indian campaign had not been successful. To the surprise of everyone, Captain West laid a charge of "dereliction of duty" against Custer. West had an axe to grind. Custer had placed one of his favourites, Cooke, in charge of the wagon train over the higher-ranking West. West was only in command of the troopers guarding the train. And earlier, at Fort Wallace, Custer had arrested West for intoxication on duty.

This wasn't the only turbulence in the Hancock's summer Indian campaign. Congress was unhappy with the amount of money being spent with little or no results. Congress set up a commission of army and civilian representatives to meet with, and negotiate with, the hostile tribes. Washington wanted assurance of safety for the railways, and to get a plan for "civilizing" the Indians.

Meanwhile Lieutenant-Colonel Custer, Brevet Major-General Custer, was forced to leave his Seventh Cavalry to await court martial.

CHAPTER 2

GEORGE ARMSTRONG CUSTER

George Armstrong Custer had come to fame very young in the Civil War. He captured the first prisoner of the Army of the Potomac and sent a famed Confederate trooper detachment into retreat. By the age of twenty-three, the less-than-brilliant student at West Point had become the youngest general in the Union army, jumping from lieutenant to brigadier-general in no time. He adopted a showman-like uniform for himself, with a broad-brimmed hat setting off long golden curls. He'd been daring and successful, was well-known to the public, and was in on the major surrender at the ending of the war.

In April of 1865, as the Civil War was drawing to a close, the United States Army had manoeuvred the Confederate General Robert E. Lee in place for a showdown in Virginia. Twenty-five-year-old Brevet Brigadier-General Custer headed a 2,300-man division of four Michigan cavalry regiments that circled the confederates at Appomattox. Custer was in the forefront awaiting word from his commander General Sheridan when, under a flag of truce, he met with an officer from the other side, James Longstreet. Custer planned to accept the surrender on behalf of Sheridan. This was a violation of military etiquette because it would undercut both Lee and the head of the army of the north, General Ulysses S. Grant — and Grant had a reputation for never forgetting such a slight. Longstreet refused Custer's suggestion.

Following the signing of surrender between General Lee and General Grant, in a house in the village of Appomattox, souvenirs were auctioned off. General Sheridan bought the small pine table which the generals had used to write the terms of surrender. This he presented to Custer for his wife Elizabeth Bacon Custer. In a letter dated April 10, 1865, from Appomattox Court House in Virginia, Sheridan wrote:

> My dear Madam — I respectfully present to you the small writing-table on which the conditions for the surrender of the Confederate Army of northern Virginia were written by Lt. General Grant — and permit me to say, Madam, that there is scarcely an individual in our service who has contributed more to bring this about than your very gallant husband.
>
> Yours very respectfully
> Phil H. Sheridan
> Major General[1]

Custer's battlefield promotion to brigadier-general was in the volunteers, the Michigan brigade, not the regular army. He had joined General Sheridan's cavalry the year before. For a young man who had graduated at the bottom of his class at West Point, he hadn't done badly. His standing at West Point was further marred by the fact that, after graduating, he was court-martialled for not stopping a fight between two cadets. He was saved from punishment because of the need for officers in the war.

Custer had done well in the war. He fought in the First Battle of Bull Run and served with distinction in Virginia and Gettysburg campaigns. At one point he set a record, taking fifty-one guns in ten days. The public loved him: his flamboyant style, the blond flowing locks, and the stylish, outrageous rebel hat he adopted. His men called him "Old Curly." He gathered around him not only members of his family — his brother Tom had joined him on the battle field in 1864 — but also a coterie of young officers, among them the Canadian William Winer Cooke.

Courtesy of Denver Public Library, Western History Collection, B58.

Portrait of Brevet Brigadier-General, Lieutenant-Colonel George Armstrong Custer, in 1865. He was the youngest general in the Union Army during the United States Civil War.

After the war, Custer made much of his leave time in Washington and elsewhere, meeting politicians, making friends, keeping in the public eye. Secretary of War Edwin M. Stanton said of him: "A gallant officer makes a gallant soldier."

May 24 and 25, 1865, were days of celebration in Washington for the victorious army of the north. Unfortunately for Sheridan, General Grant had already sent him to keep an eye on Mexico, fearing some interference from the French who had supported the southern cause. But the victorious Custer rode his white horse up Pennsylvania Avenue, to the cheering of the crowds.

Later on, President Johnson decided the country should be reunited by a political tour, with speeches at strategic places. The Custers were invited to join the presidential party. George Armstrong Custer took along his wife Elizabeth "Libbie" Bacon Custer, whom he'd married in a society wedding in Monroe, Michigan.

Custer had built up a certain celebrity during and after the Civil War. At the same time he made enemies; those who saw his weaker side. He had been court-martialled once and would be again. He was considered by some to be foppish and conceited. He was puritanical in his social mores; abstaining from alcohol and swearing and encouraging others to do the same. At the same time he didn't really believe in organized religion.

After the war, Custer returned to the regular army as captain and was assigned to Texas for a time. In 1866 he was promoted to lieutenant-colonel in the Seventh Cavalry, which had been formed the year before and assigned to Fort Riley, Kansas. Custer then began his career as an Indian fighter. Now, two years later, he was facing a second, more serious, court martial.

CHAPTER 3

CUSTER'S COURT MARTIAL

B Y THE TIME THE COURT CONVENED, A COUPLE OF CHANGES
had occurred. General Hancock had been replaced by General
Philip Sheridan as commander of the Missouri district, and the trial
had been moved from Fort Riley, Kansas, to Fort Leavenworth,
Kansas, one of the best posts in the west.

The Custers received a great deal of support through the mail, particularly from the various garrisons of the army in the west. They also
heard from friends from as far east as Washington, D.C. Custer picked
a close associate, Captain Charles C. Parsons, Fourth U.S. Artillery, as
lawyer for the defence. Parsons was a West Point classmate, had received
his commission the same time as Custer, and had a good record as a
military lawyer. Parsons was also from Custer's state of Ohio.

The court martial, by order of the commanding general Ulysses
S. Grant at Washington, D.C., opened September 15, 1867, at 11 a.m.
It was composed of ten army officers. It immediately adjourned to
the next morning. There was a fuss about seniority of rank and voting
order that was finally settled out of Washington by telegraph. This
issue came back to haunt the court later with an almost comic flurry
of telegraph messages and changing of minds about the ranking —
the whole thing being confused by the two series of ranks, army and
volunteer or "brevet." Objections over one member of the court were
resolved by allowing that member to withdraw at his own request.
Then the court settled in.

The formality of the specific charges was outlined with the list
of witnesses, officers, and troopers, to be called. There were three

charges. The first: absence without leave from his command. It was stated Custer did, at or near Fort Wallace, Kansas, "absent himself from his command without proper authority, and proceed to Fort Harker, Kansas, a distance of about 275 miles, this at a time when his command was expected to be actively engaged against hostile Indian."

The second charge was conduct prejudice to good order and military discipline. This addressed the issue of his troops having just completed a long and exhausting march to get to Fort Wallace. It said the horses were not rested and were in unfit condition. It alleged Custer took three commissioned officers and about seventy-five men with their horses in a "rapid march" from Fort Wallace to Fort Hays, "upon private business and without authority," seriously affecting the public interest by over-marching and damaging horses belonging to his command.

The third charge concerned the situation at Downer Station when, after learning Indians had attacked a small party detached from his escort, he failed to take measures to repulse the Indians, and after learning that two men had been killed, he did not pursue the Indians or recover the bodies.[1]

The incident involving the deserters came back to haunt Custer during the court martial. The second charge of "conduct prejudicial to good order and military discipline" not only dealt with the Fort Wallace issue but also with the previous Platte River incident of July 7, 1867.

The charge specified that Custer, "when ordering a party of three commissioned officers and others in pursuit of supposed deserters who were then in view of leaving camp, *also order* the said party to shoot the supposed deserters down dead, and to bring none in alive."

This charge stated that he ordered the following troopers of his regiment — Bugler Barney Tolliver of Company K, Private Charles Johnson of Company K, Private Alburger of Company D, and other enlisted men of his command — *to be shot down* as supposed deserters, but without trial; and caused three men to be severely wounded.

The charge also said that Custer put the men in a government wagon to travel eighteen miles, refusing to allow them medical treatment. Johnson subsequently died ten days later, and the fourth charge was that Custer caused his death.[2]

Custer pleaded "not guilty" to all charges.

Captain Louis Hamilton began his testimony at 10 a.m., September 17, 1867. He said that the regiment had been at Fort Wallace only a day before a detachment of about seventy-five men left for Fort Harker. Under prosecution questioning he said the detail was to "escort Gen, Custer," and the horses were in "very bad condition." The questioning centred on the speed of the march from Fort Wallace to Fort Hays, with about five hours' rest. He said the "marching was continuous but not rapid." It was 150 miles from Fort Wallace to the stopping point at Big Creek, and the rests were intermittent.

When asked to state more explicitly the condition of the horses, Captain Hamilton maintained that the horses "were not fit for immediate service. They were exhausted," when they reached Big Creek, near Fort Hays.

Next the prosecutor focused on the Indian attack on a small detail of men. Indians had killed two of the men and wounded one of the horses. Captain Hamilton gave damning testimony regarding Custer's action. He said Custer didn't order any pursuit of the Indians.

> Q: Was any action taken for the pursuit of the Indians?

> A: No sir.

> Q: Were any measures taken by Gen. Custer to recover the bodies of the men reported wounded and dead?

A: None that I know of.

Q: How soon after that report spoken of, reached you, did Gen. Custer leave?

A: In about three-fourths of an hour or an hour.

Q: On his way to the east?

A: Yes sir.[3]

On cross examination by the defence, Captain Hamilton testified that at Downer Station he applied to Custer to "halt the command," but Custer refused. This was after the small detail came in to report the Indian attack. Hamilton wanted to stop at Downer Station since there were Indians in the neighbourhood.

Q: When you asked Gen. Custer to make a longer halt at Downer's Station, what reply did he make?

A: He said he would have to go along.[4]

There was a pause in testimony as the court dealt with some technical matters regarding the membership, then it met on Sunday, September 22, 1867, with Lieutenant William W. Cooke being called as a witness by the prosecution.

William Winer Cooke was considered a handsome man — six feet tall, heavy set. But it was his long, flowing whiskers that really set him apart in the looks category. They hung from his side cheeks, not from the chin, touching the third row of buttons on his dress tunic. They were called Dundrearies, after pompous Lord Dundreary from the play *Our American Cousin*. This was the comedy President

Abraham Lincoln went to see at the Ford Theatre in Washington, the night he was shot by an assassin.

Cooke became close friends with Tom Custer, Lieutenant-Colonel Custer's younger brother, making him a member of the "Custer Clan." Cooke and the young Custer had served in the same area during the Civil War and were in the area of the Appomattox Courthouse in Virginia when the surrender was signed by the south. It seems likely Cooke met Tom Custer, also a junior officer, first, and through him became acquainted with Custer while he was a Civil War brevet major-general.

Cooke was a deadly shot with both carbine and pistol; he led the regiment's sharpshooters. Cooke was also one of the fastest runners in the regiment. That might not seem relevant, but athletic prowess counted since athletic contests were often the only entertainment at the forts on the western front. This didn't mean he was universally liked. Some of the troopers who weren't his fans called him "The Queen's Own," possibly a reference to his Canadian roots.

Cooke's reckoning of the timing from Fort Wallace to Big Creek was a little different than Hamilton's. Cooke said it was a fifty-seven hour march, and they'd halted "at least 10 hours" throughout the trip. He said he wasn't aware of the condition of the horses since he spent his time getting mules for General Custer for use on the ambulance wagon.

At one o'clock that afternoon, Custer, Cook, and Tom Custer left for Harker in an ambulance wagon drawn by four mules. Cooke testified they made it in twelve hours. Then Custer went on to Fort Riley by train. The prosecutor asked the Canadian about the Indian attack in the area of Downer Station and what action Custer took. He said he did not hear any report made directly to Custer about the attack.

Q: Do you know whether any of the command of Gen. Custer or any detachment from the command were sent out for the relief of the detachment?

A: I do not know of any being sent.

Q: Do you know whether any measures were taken
to pursue the Indians, by Gen. Custer?

A: No sir; it was considered inexpedient to pursue
the Indians that distance, as that had happened to
those men some two or three hours before.[5]

The ambulance wagon left Downer Station half an hour after the
report came in. Cooke was cross-examined by the defence about the
reason he left Fort Wallace in the first place.

Q: What authority did Gen. Custer give you to
leave Fort Wallace; verbal or written?

A: Verbal. I went with him.

Q: Did he say why you were going?

A: There was no commissary stores at Fort Wallace,
and I was going down to bring up a train (wagon
train) of supplies for the Post. This is what I understood was the cause of my going down.[6]

Custer's defence then tried to have some of the testimony by
Cooke dismissed as "irrelevant," in particular that any reference to
ambulances not taken at Fort Hays be expunged. This request was
not granted.

The testimony that followed centred on the original verbal
orders given to Custer by Lieutenant-General William T. Sherman
for his expedition to make the circle from Fort Hays to the Platte
River and south to Fort Wallace. He was to "hunt out and chastise

the Cheyennes and that portion of the Sioux who are their allies between the Smoky Hill and the Platte." And to avoid a "collision" with friendly bands.

Documents were presented to the court that showed Custer had orders to make Fort Wallace a base, and if need be to get supplies at Fort Hays. He was not to use a wagon train but to use pack saddles. Some crucial testimony from Lieutenant Thomas B. Weir, adjutant with the Seventh Cavalry, indicated Custer received these orders before he got to Fort Harker. Weir testified there was no record on the books at Headquarters of the District of Upper Arkansas of any leave of absence for General Custer during the month of July, 1867. He said that as Acting Assistant Adjutant General of the District to the Upper Arkansas, he knew of no "leave of absence, verbal or written" given to Custer.

> Q: Do you know by the records at your head-
> quarters whether any authority was given to the
> accused to be present at, or to proceed to, Fort
> Harker from his command?

> A: There is none on record in that office.[7]

Captain Arthur B. Carpenter of the Thirty-Seventh Infantry was questioned at length about the Seventh Cavalry detail that was attacked by Indians. It was Carpenter and his men who brought in the body of the trooper and the wounded man. He said Custer didn't help but proceeded to the next stop, Downer Station. Carpenter admitted to the defence it would not have made sense to try to chase the Indians. "It would have been fruitless," since they were long gone by then.

Sergeant James Connelly of Company D testified that he was in the rear of the command and often had to "pick up stragglers" and often the horses could go no farther and had to be left at different stations during the march. Three horses were shot because of their poor condition. He testified that he expected to join the command soon, "expected every ravine [he] passed to see the command while Indians were in pursuit of [them]."

Connelly was then questioned closely by defence lawyer Parsons on two points: if Connelly was sure the man had been wounded and not killed, and if Custer actually heard his report on the Indian attack when he got to Downer Station.

Q: How far was the accused from Capt. Hamilton when you reported?

A: He might be 40 or 50 yards or so; I don't know exactly. After I reported to Capt. Hamilton as I passed by the station door, I saw him (Custer) sitting inside the door.[8]

On September 25 came the testimony of Colonel Andrew J. Smith, commander of the District of Upper Arkansas, stationed at Fort Harker. Colonel Smith told the court martial that he had not given the accused, Custer, any leave of absence or authority to leave his command during the month of July. And he hadn't given any authority to Custer to march from Fort Wallace to Fort Hays.

Smith did admit that he made no objection when, at Fort Harker, Custer came to him and said he was going on to Fort Riley. Fort Riley was where Mrs. Custer was staying. When cross-examined by the defence, Smith said it was the middle of the night when Custer came to his quarters and he thought Custer had come by stage. When he learned the next morning that there was a command of seventy-five men and an ambulance involved, he ordered Custer back to Fort Harker.

Next up was Lieutenant Tom Custer, brother of the accused. Lieutenant Custer was examined closely on the issue of the deserter incident about twelve miles from the Platte River on July 7.

Q: State the exact language of the order as you received it, in regard to shooting those deserters if you can remember it?

A: The accused spoke to me and said, "I want you to get on your horse and go after those deserters and shoot them down." That is as near as I can recollect it....

Q: State what occurred after you received that order and started in pursuit of the deserters?

A: I saw the men laying down their arms and Maj. Elliott and Lt. Cook [sic] rode toward them. One of the men, I think it was a man named Johnson ran to get his carbine and a man named Atkins, a scout who as along with the party — I don't know whether he had orders or not — up [sic] to the man and said he would blow his brains out if he attempted to touch his carbine. In the meantime I saw Maj. Elliott and Lt. Cook firing on them. By that time I was with them myself and we fired on them.[9]

The defence came back through questioning to show there had been desertions the night before, at least ten from one company, but none after the shooting incident. Also, answering questions from the court, Tom Custer seemed to further testify against his brother by indicating Major Elliott and the Canadian, Lieutenant Cooke, fired on the troopers after the troopers had laid down their arms; that this occurred because they were carrying out the orders of his brother, Lieutenant-Colonel Custer.

The defence once more argued against procedures of the court, particularly since it didn't want the Canadian recalled. But the

Judge Advocate ruled against the defence, and Cooke was recalled as a witness for the prosecution. It was the second charge to do with the deserters' incident.

Cooke testified that, in regard to the deserters, Custer ordered him "to pursue and shoot them down." He said the men were ordered to halt and surrender, then Elliott made a motion with his carbine "which I think brought on the shooting." He also testified the deserters had at least three carbines in hand. He said he didn't know whether or not the wounded men, who were placed in a wagon, received any medical treatment.

Custer was confident at this stage that he would be exonerated of the charges. He wrote to his friend Mr. Walker:

> I have obtained evidence that, last spring, when desertions were so numerous, General Hancock telegraphed General Sheridan to shoot deserters down. Genl. Sheridan has been summoned to testify that he ordered me to shoot without trial for the same offence. He himself drew my attention to this and urged me to introduce it in evidence.
>
> He assured me that in any and all circumstances I could count him as my friend, and that, further, the authorities in Washington regard my trial as an attempt by Hancock to cover up the failures of the Indian expedition.
>
> West is drinking himself to death, has delirium tremens, to such an extent the Prosecution will not put him on the witness stand.[10]

The morning of September 26, the prosecution called Dr. I.T. Coates, Acting Assistant Surgeon with the Seventh Cavalry, to the stand. He testified that a six-mule wagon came into camp with the three wounded deserters aboard. He said that when the wagon first came in he and some others started toward it, but then Custer told him "not to go near those men at that time. I stood of course. I obeyed his orders."

After about two hours he did give them medical attention, and that was the same as he would give on the battlefield: opiate and making them comfortable. Dr. Coates testified that Barney Tolliver, the bugler, had a flesh wound in the arm. The second man, Alburger, had a flesh wound in the shoulder, another in the ribs, and on his finger. But it was Johnson who suffered the worst injury: a flesh wound in the side, and a bullet apparently hit him in the left side of his forehead coming out under the jaw, entering again the upper part of the chest. Dr. Coates said the "ball" or bullet entered the left temple and came out below in a direct line. He was asked to indicate how he thought this could occur, and the doctor answered: "The shooter must have been some distance above him, I should judge. The shooter must have been mounted, for the ball having taken that direction."[11]

Dr. Coates said he did not dress the wounds for two days, about 180 miles on the trail, because there was only muddy water from the buffalo wallows, and he dressed them once they came to a stream of clear water. Johnson died of his wounds about ten days later at Fort Wallace.

Under cross-examination by the accused, the doctor said that Custer ordered him to give the deserters medical attention once in camp and that he, the doctor, had command of the wagon in which they rode, and he testified that Johnson did not die in consequence of any order given by the accused in regard to medical attention. A member of the court raised the issue of what did the doctor understand the accused to mean when he directed the doctor not to attended the men immediately when they were brought in.

Dr. Coates said he thought the objection was made for effect: "There had been a great many deserters — some 30 or 40 the night previous, and the men were crowding around the wagon, and I had an idea the General wished to make an impression on the men that they would be dealt with in the severest and harshest manner."[12]

He said it was by Custer's order that he finally gave medical assistance, and it was really half an hour or an hour after they were brought in. No further prosecution witnesses arrived at Leavenworth, although they had been summoned, so the court turned to the defence.

CHAPTER 4

COURT MARTIAL CONTINUED

O N September 27, 1867, with still no new prosecution witnesses in sight, the Judge Advocate introduced the original report written by the accused, Custer. It was his report of the march from the Platte River to Fort Wallace and subsequently to Fort Harker. It told of how thirty-five men had deserted in twenty-four hours near the Platte River and how another thirteen deliberately shouldered arms and headed out in broad daylight. Custer was concerned that, since they would be camping out that night and might lose more to desertion, his command would be in jeopardy, unsafe.

> I directed Major Elliott, Lieutenants Custer, Cooke, and Jackson with a few of the guard to pursue the deserters who were still visible although more than a mile distant, and to bring the dead bodies of as many as could be taken back to camp ... the wounds received by those referred to above, did not prove serious, I regret to say, but the effect upon the command was all that could be desired. Not a single desertion took place from that time so long as I remained with command.[1]

He offered a further explanation regarding the deserters:

> My march from Fort Wallace to Fort Harker was made without incident except the killing of two

men about five miles beyond Downer's Station. A sergeant and six men had been sent back to bring up a man who had halted at the last ranch; when returning, this party was attacked by between forty and fifty Indians, and two of them were killed. Had they offered any defence this would not have occurred, instead however they put spurs to their horses and endeavored to escape by flight.[2]

There were delays because of prosecution witnesses from Fort Hays who never arrived and because Custer had a boil. On Saturday, October 5, Major Elliott was called as witness for the prosecution. He testified that when he rode out after the deserters, just as he started out, Custer said, "I want you to shoot them." Elliott said Charles Johnson of Company K raised a carbine as if to shoot him. Elliott said he was riding at a gallop and rode to the trooper. Johnson threw down his carbine. He was shot after that.

Elliot also testified that the horses were not in condition to take on another march of a hundred or so miles when they arrived at Fort Wallace. He was left in command at Fort Wallace when Custer headed out with his seventy-five men.

The defence indicated to the court it was relying on testimony from its first witness, Lieutenant-General William T. Sherman, since it was anticipated the accused would not have to bring forward any other witnesses. Court resumed Monday, October 7, but it was the accused's younger brother, Lieutenant Tom Custer, not General Sherman, who was first witness for the defence. He said that at a dinner in June, General Sherman had indicated Custer could do anything he wanted in going after the Indians.

Lieutenant Cooke was then recalled as a witness for the defence. Cooke testified he was at that same dinner on the Platte River, June 16, with Sherman and Custer. The testimony indicated Sherman was giving Custer a free hand in his command and not to pay too much attention to restrictions that might be set by General Auger.

Q: State as near as you can the exact language employed by Gen. Sherman to the accused.

A: He made the remark that he would receive orders from the Gen. Augur, but not to restrict himself to any orders. He made the remark that he (Custer) could go to hell if he wanted to.

Q: Did he state that he could go to any special post?

A: He said he could go to any post he chose.

Q: Did he name any particular post?

A: No sir, I think not.

Q: Did he say anything about the orders Gen. Augur had received restricting him?

A: Yes sir, he said Gen. Augur would not interfere with him to any extent.

Q: Did he (Sherman) intimate any extreme western post the accused could go to?

A: During the conversation he made the remark that he (Custer) could go to Denver if he wished.[3]

S.N. Harper, the wagon master, told the court he didn't sleep all the night of July 6 because men were trying to steal stock and desert.

They even told him what their intentions were. And he told Custer about it in the morning. The quarter master sergeant Peter McMahon testified to the same, that it was generally known the men were going to desert. He said the shooting of the deserters prevented any further such action.

Dr. Coates, who was recalled to testify for the defence, said he was told not to let the men know he was treating the deserters.

Custer wished to recall Major Elliott, but since he was called back to Fort Harker his deposition was submitted in which he explained his actions in volunteering to go after the deserters:

He was afraid that, owing to the slowness of the guard, the deserters would escape, further, that it was his [Elliott's] opinion that the effect of the order to pursue and shoot the said alleged deserters was good upon the whole command and that had the attempt at desertion been successful, at least one fourth of the command were likely, on that night, to desert.[4]

Elliott also testified that, since General Hancock was not at Fort Wallace, Custer had decided to go to Fort Harker, or the nearest telegraph station, to report and get further orders. The Judge Advocate conceded that Custer hadn't received the orders because of the killing of Lieutenant Kidder who was carrying the orders. Then the certified copy of the orders was submitted to the court. They showed that, on June 27, he was ordered to go to Fort Wallace and report to Hancock, and July 16 was told, "you are not restricted in your movements to the vicinity of Fort Wallace, but are to operate wherever the presence of movements to Indians may lead you."

Submitted on behalf of the defence were various orders by Hancock, dated earlier in the year, indicating his orders to "kill or capture the deserters."

Tom Custer was recalled by the defence. He testified that ten men in his company had deserted on July 6, one day before the incident in question. Even one of the non-commissioned officers deserted.

Captain Louis Hamilton was recalled for the defence. He had doubled the stable guard that night but still lost nine men. On several occasions men broke through the guard.

The Canadian, Cooke, was recalled to testify about Custer checking out mail stages from Fort Wallace to Big Creek.

Q: Did he search the mails?

A: Yes sir.

Q: For what object?

A: To obtain any orders there might be in reference to his movements. We had had no mail for about a month.

Q: Did he make any inquiries of any trains he met?

A: Yes sir.[5]

A number of officers were called to testify that it was not unusual for officers to ride in ambulances in making trips on the plains. And there were no orders against the practice. Officers were called to prove that Custer had taken a number of lesser measures to prevent desertion, including bringing deserters to trial and doubling guards. A statement from record books submitted to the court showed 156 men had deserted from the Seventh Cavalry between April 19 and July 13, 1867.

Captain Thomas Weir of the Seventh testified that he was called to Colonel Smith's quarters in the middle of the night where Custer was. Captain Weir testified that Smith knew about Fort Riley because he sent a message with Custer: "Give my respects to the ladies."

At 10 a.m. on Friday, October 11, Captain Parson read the written defence. In answer to the charge of absence without leave, it stated that the first stage — Fort Wallace to Fort Harker — Custer was on "urgent public business." It said Custer went on to Fort Riley to see Mrs. Custer with the knowledge of his commanding officer, Colonel Smith. The statement said Custer had verbal orders from General Sherman in June, then a written order that was eventually lost. Custer emphasized the instructions left him with movements "almost discretionary with myself." Parsons argued that with the confusion of orders, and those lost by Kidder's death, that Custer felt he was to report to General Hancock whether at "Wallace or wherever or Harker … the accused felt it to be his duty in the absence of other orders to follow General Hanock to Fort Harker or the nearest telegraph station to report to him and ascertain what orders were for him." The defence lawyer said Custer emphasized the need for supplies at Fort Wallace as well.

Regarding the trip from Fort Harker to Fort Riley, Custer said he reported to Smith in the middle of the night upon arrival at Fort Harker. He said he wanted to visit his family at Fort Riley: "Gen. Smith accompanied us out the door and in recognition of what I have said told me to remember him to my family at Riley…." Custer said he didn't call Smith for the defence because it was obvious Smith had been awakened from sleep; his recollection was indistinct, and "a brooding pestilence hanging over Harker" caused Smith anxiety.

Regarding the attack on a small party of his command near Downer Station, Custer claimed he knew nothing about it until it was over.

On the issue of the deserters, the order to Lieutenant Jackson "to bring none alive" was only for discipline effect on the troopers, and the fact Jackson sent some deserters back immediately under guard proves that. "He [Jackson] understood well what it meant and that it was done for necessary effect upon the men and that it did not contemplate anything inhuman ..."

Custer referred to the telegrams of the previous winter, from Major-General Hancock, relating to the phrase "Capture or kill" (the Indians). Custer said he didn't use his six-year record of service to the country in the Civil War to bolster his case, but if he had done so, it would show.

> Through six years which I have tried honestly and faithfully to devote to my country and to all, in my judgment, that was honourable and useful my profession. I have never been once absent from my command without leave as here charged. I have never wearied or in any way made use of my men for the advancement of my private wishes or interests — as here charged, or severely tasked any living creature as here charged, except under a sense of duty.[6]

Captain Chandler, as Judge Advocate, read out his final argument. He emphasized that the charge of absent without leave referred to when Custer actually left Fort Wallace, not just Fort Harker, for Fort Riley in the middle of the night. He, Custer, was to be "actively engaged against hostile Indians." The issue of why Colonel Smith didn't stop Custer in the middle of the night at Fort Harker was not clearly addressed.

Chandler argued against the various orders that Custer "assumed," but in fact did not receive; for example, the one Lieutenant Kidder was carrying when attacked and killed. The Judge Advocate referred to testimony of the forced march of fifty-seven hours from the Platte River to Wallace and the poor condition of horses onward to Fort Harker. He quoted Sergeant Connelly who testified that he had to pick up stragglers at the back of the march and that they had to leave horses at various stations; several were abandoned and left on the prairie, and three were shot. Only about forty-five or fifty of the men out of the seventy-five escort detail were mounted by the time they arrived at Big Creek.

The Judge Advocate weighed in heavily on charges relating to the shooting of deserters and the refusal of immediate medical treatment.

And so, on October 11, 1867, the court found Brevet General G.A. Custer, Lieutenant-Colonel of the Seventh Cavalry, guilty on five charges, excepting the neglect and refusal to allow the deserters medical treatment.

Custer was suspended from rank and command for one year. He also lost a year's pay.

There was still the review to come, and three days later the entire transcript was submitted to the adjutant-general.

Then-Lieutenant-General Sherman, who never did turn up for the court martial as a witness for the defence, issued a statement that the "proceedings, findings and sentence in the case of Brevet Major General Custer are approved by General Grant ... in which the levity of the sentence, considering the nature of the offenses of Bvt. Major General Custer if found guilty, is to be remarked on." (Custer was actually a brevet lieutenant-general). A Leavenworth newspaper later quoted Assistant Adjutant-General E.D. Townsend, who was "convinced that the Court, in awarding so lenient a sentence for the offenses of which the accused if found guilty, must have taken into consideration his previous record."

Major-General Sheridan was in New York when the sentence came down. Although never appearing on behalf of Custer, it was known that Custer was his favourite. Custer himself, who believed that the evidence didn't merit the verdict, later wrote to his friend Mr. Walker, "I have written to General Sheridan to make no effort to obtain a remission of any portion of my sentence. I would not accept it."[7]

The controversy over the court martial continued in the press; the general opinion was that the cruelty to his troopers, in the desertion charge, was of more importance than the absence without leave. Newspapers in the mid-west picked up the trial and took sides on the sentencing. The Sandusky Ohio *Daily Register* defended Custer. It dismissed the charges brought by General Hancock and said that four of the eight members of the court were inferior in rank to the accused, which was against the 75th Article of War. The newspaper said one member of the court was a commissary who had been censured by Custer for corruption in issuing rations.

Custer wrote that the charge of cruelty was near an acquittal since the phrase "and attaches no criminality thereto" was added.

General Sheridan gave the Custers his suite at Fort Leavenworth. Custer settled down to his fate and began writing his autobiography.

But it wasn't over yet. Just after New Year's Day of 1869 there was a new trial to contend with. The *Daily Conservative* reported the arrest of Brevet Lieutenant-General Custer and Lieutenant William W. Cooke:

> On a charge of murdering one Johnson, a soldier, who it is claimed was shot by Cook [sic] under orders from Custar [sic] in Colorado Territory near Fort Sedgwick, Nebraska, on the 7th of July last. Constable Kirkham and Deputy Stillwell served the warrant, and the prisoners came down from the Fort last evening and gave bonds in the sum of $1,000 each for their appearance for examination on Wednesday, the 8th inst., before Justice Adams. A. J. Smith and Surgeon M. Madison Mills are their bondsmen.[8]

The case began on January 8. The defence immediately put a motion to dismiss the case on the grounds of informalities, questioning the jurisdiction of Justice Adams. The motion was granted and the prisoners discharged. But hours later a new complaint was laid, and the two were re-arrested and a new trial begun.

One of the deserters from Company K, Clement Willis, gave testimony against Lieutenant Cooke. Willis said he was ten steps from Johnson when he saw Lieutenant Cooke shoot him with a revolver. Willis said Johnson was shot in the arm, and fell to his knees, begging not to be killed. He testified Cooke shot Johnson in the head. He said Johnson then begged Cooke to kill him. Willis said he visited Johnson every day until his death on July 16.

On January 19, 1868, the Leavenworth *Daily Conservative* took Custer to task for his appeal to the public through the press, particularly the letter to the Sandusky, Ohio, *Register*, in which Custer criticized the composition of the court. The *Daily Conservative* said this:

> General Custer illustrates the danger of putting upon a man more honor and responsibility than he can carry.... He had a great deal of "dash," that gave him popularity, because officers less in rank, and men equal in valor, generously paid the penalty of his rashness, and redeemed his mistakes with the dogged valor of true soldiers....
>
> We regretted his becoming a political prostitute in the harem of (president) Andrew Johnson. We regret his military disgrace, and would not have aided its publicity had he not forced himself upon the press.[9]

These charges were eventually dismissed, and in June of 1868, Custer and Libbie left for Monroe, Michigan, since his comrades in the Seventh Cavalry were heading out for the summer campaigns and he couldn't be part of them. Those campaigns were not successful. The Seventh and some infantry fought a losing battle against the combined forces of Cheyennes, Kiowas, and Arapahos near Camp Supply.

Then, on September 24, 1868, Custer received the following telegram:

HEADQUARTERS DEPARTMENT OF THE MISSOURI, IN THE FIELD, FORT HAYS, KANSAS, SEPTEMBER 24, 1868

To General GA. Custer, Monroe, Michigan
Generals Sherman, Sully and myself, and nearly all the officers of your regiment have asked for you and I hope the applications will be successful. Can you come at once? Eleven companies of your regiment will move about the first of October against the hostile Indians, from Medicine Lodge Creek toward the Wichita mountains.

Signed F.P.H. Sheridan
Major General Commanding[10]

Custer left by train the next day and arrived at Fort Hays the morning of September 30. His regiment was already near the Arkansas River southeast of Fort Dodge. He wrote home to Libbie on October 4, "I breakfasted with Genl. Sheridan and staff. He said, 'Custer, I rely on you in everything, and shall send you on this expedition without orders, leaving you to act entirely on your own judgment.'"[11]

Several days after his arrival at camp, it was attacked by Indians. The Washita Campaign had begun.

CHAPTER 5

WILLIAM WINER COOKE

THE LEAD SHARPSHOOTER FOR THE SEVENTH CAVALRY, Canadian William Winer Cooke, was just sixteen when he moved to the United States in 1862, sent to stay with relatives across the border. Cooke grew up in the small village of Mount Pleasant in southwestern Upper Canada, a privileged youth in a prominent family. It was an apparent indiscretion in his teenage years that set Cooke on the path leading to a friendship with George Armstrong Custer.

Mount Pleasant sits on the Grand River just five miles south of Brant's Ford, as the river made its last miles to Lake Erie. The site was of strategic importance after the American Revolution of 1776. A number of Iroquois Confederacy fought on the British side, and because this put them in a precarious position in the new Republic they were given lands on each side of the Grand River in British North America.

Joseph Brant, one of the Confederacy leaders, actively sought Americans to settle within the granted lands. Immigrants came from Pennsylvania, as well as New York State. One of them was Abraham Cooke, a twenty-four-year-old plasterer who emigrated from New York in 1815. He soon built himself a successful merchandising business. Abraham Cooke was considered a "merchant prince." He had a prominent position in Mount Pleasant as storekeeper, postmaster, and member of the Bethesda Chapel, then the Anglican Church. He married Eleanor Hardy who had good connections to the founding families; their home became a social centre.

By the 1840s, spurred on by the wheat economy, Mount Pleasant saw a spurt of grand homes, even mansions, being built. An impressive example was that of the Cookes. Builders brought in from Hamilton created the Georgian-style, red-brick home with its Greek Revival and Regency touches; a spectacular showy mansion. The 1851 census described it as a "2 storey brick castle," while an Ellis descendant in 1916 called it "a palatial residence for those days ... beautifully appointed and was justly esteemed as now one of the show places of the district."[1]

There were six fireplaces and two huge pillars supporting the second storey. The kitchen was equipped with ovens capable of baking fifty loaves of bread. Each year Abraham Cooke invited the school children to the widow's walk at the top of the house to see the view of Brantford in the distance.

A major occasion was the visit by the new Governor General James Bruce, Lord Elgin, in September of 1849 — a week-long event that included officers from the London garrison and distinguished guests from Toronto. In appreciation, the governor general gave his name to the new mansion, "Brucefield." The visit was not all a bed of roses. The hostility between Tories and Reformers, exacerbated by the 1837 Rebellion, still continued. There were rumours of threats

Brucefield, Mount Pleasant, Upper Canada, now Ontario, home of Abraham and Eleanor Cooke, grandparents of William Winer Cooke.

Courtesy of Jim Butler.

against Elgin who had signed the Rebellion Losses Bill that spring, giving compensation to property owners during the Lower Canada Rebellion, many of whom were rebels themselves. Angry crowds had burned the parliament buildings of the United Canadas in Montreal. A Hamilton paper referred to Abraham Cooke as a radical, and some reports indicated he "supplied rebels from his store" during the Rebellion in Upper Canada.

By the 1840s, Abraham and Eleanor had three sons. The elder son, Alexander Hardy Cooke, married Angelina Augusta Winer, member of a prominent family in Hamilton. They set up house in the Cooke family's original single-storey clay-and-plaster home. Alec was a medical doctor. They had three sons, the eldest of which died. The oldest surviving son, born in 1846, was William, or Willie as he was affectionately called.

Willie and his friends attended the elementary school in Mount Pleasant, then moved on to high school in Brantford, travelling five miles by sleigh in winter. The village boys soon earned a reputation among the "town boys" for their impressive wrestling prowess. Willie took that athletic prowess with him to the Seventh Cavalry.

The influence of American phrenologist Orson Fowler, who promoted the octagonal building design, was felt in Ontario at that time, including in Mount Pleasant. The village soon had three octagonal buildings, including a private school for young gentlemen called the Nelles Academy. It was built on Abraham Cooke's land. The building was three storeys, the first and second used for classrooms of the non-denominational high school. Professor W.W. Nelles, who had been teaching in the United States, was installed as headmaster. The wealthy, or "aristocracy," of the area sent their boys to this academy. Young Willie Cooke attended classes right on his grandfather's turf. And so Willie grew up in this privileged setting; eldest son of the eldest son, cushioned by wealth and family background.

But around the age of sixteen, Willie was suddenly enrolled in a private school in Buffalo, New York. The story was that he had fathered an illegitimate child of a less socially prominent neighbour's daughter, and so was removed from the scene.

The Civil War was on. The next year, at seventeen, Willie Cooke lied about his age, saying he was twenty-two, and joined the Twenty-Fourth New York Volunteer Cavalry in January of 1863. His grandfather had some influence on his military career, but young Cooke also proved to be worthy of the promotions. In April of 1864, he joined the Ninth Army Corps under General Ambrose E. Burnside and fought in several battles around Richmond, Virginia. He injured a leg at Petersburg and ended up in the hospital. He later rejoined his regiment at the Battle of Five Forks. He was commissioned a second lieutenant and served with the Twenty-Fourth New York Volunteer Cavalry until the end of the Civil War the next year. Cooke was wounded by a shell fragment, promoted to first lieutenant in December, and honourably mustered out in June of 1865.

More honours came later, related to his service in the Civil War. The promotions were all for "gallant and meritorious service" in the volunteer army; first as captain for service in the Battle of Petersburg, Virginia, June 17, 1864; then as major for the Battle of Dinwiddie Court House in Virginia in the spring of 1865; and then to lieutenant-colonel for service in the Battle of Sayler's Creek in Virginia in April of 1865.

With the American Civil War over, Cooke was mustered out of the U.S. volunteer army on June 25, 1865. His commission in the Seventh Cavalry was dated July 1866, but he didn't actually join the regiment until November of that year.

He spent the intervening summer back home in Mount Pleasant. It was at this time that Upper Canada faced a threat from the Fenian Raids across the border. The Fenian Brotherhood was an Irish nationalist freedom organization that planned to free Ireland from British control by attacking British North America. The Fenians attacked mostly in the Maritimes and the Niagara area. In May of 1866, 800 invaders were reported to have crossed at Buffalo. And as in the War of 1812, Mount Pleasant heeded the call to arms. An infantry company was already in place. Willie Cooke, probably relishing

Portrait of William Winer Cooke in the uniform of the Seventh Cavalry, United States Army. Cooke was born in Mount Pleasant, Upper Canada, now Ontario.

the diversion from the dull lot of helping on the farm, helped form a troop of cavalry in the village, putting them through the drills. His father, Dr. Alexander Cooke, wrote to the British Garrison in Canada, offering the troop's services. But as it turned out, none of this was needed since the British regular troops pushed the Fenians back across the border.[2]

Cooke had some high-powered connections in Washington, D.C., where he could try to find a place for himself in one of the regiments being formed to pave the way for opening up the western plains to settlers. There, in the capital, was an aunt whose husband was a lobbyist and army contractor. That influence would help his career.

The Seventh Cavalry of the United States Army was formed in 1866, a year after the end of the Civil War, and assigned to Fort Riley, Kansas. Cooke, who had turned twenty years old two months before, signed up for the Seventh as second lieutenant on July 28, 1866, the same month as Custer's appointment as head of the regiment.

Cooke arrived at Fort Riley to join the regiment November 16, the same day as Tom Custer, George Armstrong Custer's younger brother. Cooke was regimental adjutant from December 8 to February 21, 1867. On July 31, he was promoted to first lieutenant. He was twenty-one years old, and George Custer was just twenty-eight, a hero of the Civil War with a flamboyant style. Cooke had a war background, family contacts, and easy assurance; the two became fast friends.

Those first years the Canadian had a number of postings and transfers, including as regimental quartermaster at Fort Larned and a posting with Company H at Fort Harker. For a week in 1868 he was commanding officer of the company. Then, on November 10, he took a special posting as commanding officer of the sharpshooter battalion formed for the Battle of Washita.

Cooke also waged battle on the political front — a bid to get a brevet rank. Brevet ranks were honorary titles awarded for conspicuous gallantry, and the highest rank held while in command of volunteers. Officers were assigned duties of their permanent rank in the army, but were addressed by the highest rank ever held. Cooke, a first lieutenant, worked the system for the brevet rank of lieutenant-colonel that he yearned for, but was then only a lowly lieutenant in the regular army.

Cooke's mother, Augusta, had some influential friends, including President Andrew Johnson. This all certainly helped Cooke along the way in his military career. In May of 1868, Augusta Cooke wrote from an address on Bridge Street in Georgetown, D.C., to President Johnson, thanking him for his promise the previous day to look into her son's military career.

A three-pronged attack finally had its success. The president and secretary of war confirmed brevet ranks of captain and major on Cooke. Still, he yearned for more. Cooke wrote to the adjutant-general of the army thanking him for the colonel's brevet, which of course he hadn't received. The letter back was addressed to Brevet Lieutenant-Colonel Cooke. And ever afterwards he signed his name with that rank. Simple as that.[3]

CHAPTER 6

DONALD MCINTOSH

THE NINETEENTH CENTURY WAS A COLOURFUL PERIOD OF
Canadian history as British-backed companies vied for the rich
rewards of the fur trapping and trading industry. The competition
was fierce for fur pelts from the Indians, in the wilderness north to
Hudson's Bay and toward the west.

The next Canadian to join the Seventh Cavalry, a year after
Cooke, was Donald McIntosh, a descendant of one of the legendary
fur traders of Canada's northwest.

His grandfather, also Donald McIntosh, had emigrated from
Scotland during the time of Closures, when the large landowners or
Lairds evicted tenants, then took over their pastures for sheep graz-
ing. The elder Donald had been the "Chief Factor," or chief trader, for
the North West Company at Fort William on Lake Superior. By 1816
he was a partner. When the two competing companies — the North
West Company and the Hudson's Bay Company — decided to merge
in 1821, Donald McIntosh retained his position with the company,
now known as the Hudson's Bay Company.

His son, John, born in 1803 by a Chippewa woman, was raised
by his aunt, Chrissy McIntosh, in Cornwall, Upper Canada. In a letter to Chrissy from Michipicotton, dated August 12, 1816, Donald
urged Chrissy to ensure that John got proper schooling so he could
become a clerk, having already spoken to a company agent about his
son: "I desired him to examine whether he (John) is qualified or not
to be a clerk. Should he find him qualified he will tell him the time he
must be at Montreal in the spring to take his passage on the canoes
(going west)...."[1]

John became a clerk at Fort William, in what is now Ontario, when he was eighteen. From 1828 to 1832 John was stationed at Long Lake where he married Charlotte Robertson, a Métis — half English, half Chippewa. Seventeen-year-old Charlotte was the daughter of a Chippewayan woman and an English Factor, Colin Robertson. Together, she and John had eight children. One of them was young Donald, born September 3, 1838, at Jasper House, in what is now Alberta. Some records show September 4, 1839. It was Donald, with his mix of Scottish and Native blood, who eventually joined the Seventh Cavalry.[2]

Young Donald's father, John McIntosh, served in a number of Hudson's Bay posts, tracking west. In 1844 he was posted to McLeod's Lake, northeast of Stuart Lake. That's when his luck ran out. He had his oldest son Archie with him, examining his nets in Lake McLeod, when killed by a shot from ambush by a member of the Sickanie tribe.

After this, with Archie's help and the sponsorship of a well known Factor, Dr. John McLaughlin, Charlotte made her way, with her large family of eight, south to the trading post at Fort Vancouver in what is now Washington state. On June 4, 1848, when Donald was nine, Charlotte and three of her children, including Donald, were confirmed in St. James Church in Vancouver, Washington state.[3]

In 1846, when the 49th Parallel became the boundary between Canada and the United States, the Hudson's Bay Company moved its headquarters to Fort Victoria, on Vancouver Island, but the McIntosh family remained in Fort Vancouver, south of the border. Five years later, at the age of thirteen, Donald moved to Oregon City, perhaps for work, since Dr. McLaughlin was living there. He then went on to Portland for a year. By this time, his brother Archie was working for the army as an interpreter at Fort Dalles, about ninety miles above Fort Vancouver on the Columbia River. In 1854, Donald also moved to Fort Dalles. At eighteen years of age, on November 13, 1856, he joined the U.S. Army Quartermaster Department at the fort as a clerk.

* * *

The United States Army arrived in Oregon in 1849 and set up a military base at Fort Dalles, overlooking a campsite used by explorers Lewis and Clark forty-four years earlier. Fort Dalles, now known as The Dalles, sat on the Columbia River in the shadow of Mount Hood, about seventy miles east of present day Portland, Oregon. This was where McIntosh first connected with the United States Army.

During the wars with the Yakama Indians, Fort Dalles served as operational headquarters. The push for control over the Native people and the ongoing land grab to accommodate the migration west had reached the northwest.

The Yakama Indians lived along the Columbia and Yakama Rivers. They were on a plateau north of the Columbia River, east of the Cascade Mountains. The Yakama had established trade with the Hudson's Bay Company, based out of Fort Vancouver and Fort Walla Walla in Washington Territory. This friendly trade relationship with the British and Métis of the Hudson's Bay Company didn't prepare them for the much different American policy as carried out by the United States Army. For the Americans these Native people were simply an impediment to settlement of the Oregon Territory — a barrier that needed to be removed.

In 1855, Donald's brother Archie was an interpreter and guide for a military command of eighty-six troops under Major Granville O. Haller, which was going after the Yakama Indians. When Major Haller was forced to retreat, pursued by a force of 1,500 Indians, Archie led them back to Fort Dalles. That year leaders in the two territories, Washington and Oregon, enacted treaties that forced the Native tribes to give up millions of acres of land and go into reservations. The Yakama ended up on the Yakama Reservation along with thirteen other tribes.

Then, ironically, gold was discovered on the Yakama Reservation, launching the Yakama Wars. In 1856 the United States Army moved in, defeating the Indians at the Battle of Four Lakes near what is now Spokane, Washington, sending the tribes to the reservations. The two-year war included the Cascades Massacre, an attack on a white settlement by the Indians. Fourteen civilians and three soldiers died. Nine Cascade Indians, including their chief, were executed for treason. Yakama chief Kamiakin fled to the colony of British Columbia, later part of Canada, but twenty-four other chiefs were hanged or shot. By 1861, Fort Dalles had been downgraded to a quartermaster's depot.

His brother's exciting adventures may have led Donald McIntosh to join the army. He served with the Quartermaster's Department of the army at Fort Dalles and at Fort Steilacoom, near Tacoma. In 1860 he was transferred to Washington, D.C., where he served as chief clerk for the assistant quartermaster-general, Colonel Daniel H. Rucker, throughout the Civil War, 1860 to 1865.[4]

Colonel Daniel Rucker had served in the army for many years, taking part in the Mexican wars in the 1840s. In 1849 he served in the Quartermaster's Department as an assistant quartermaster, on duty during the California Gold Rush. For twelve years he set up provision depots of horses and men to relieve emigrants travelling west. Much of this time he was in New Mexico.

The Quartermaster's Department in Washington was a huge operation during the Civil War, and Rucker was recognized for his unusual ability to oversee it. At the beginning of the Civil War, Rucker was offered a post as major with the Sixth Cavalry, but turned that down. He became a major in the Quartermaster's Department on August 3, 1861, and a colonel on September 28, 1861. On May 23, 1863, Rucker was promoted to brigadier-general of the volunteers and the United States Army "for diligent and faithful service" and "faithful and meritorious service." He was in charge of the procurement and distribution of wagons, horses, ambulances, mules, harnesses and forage, and countless other items to keep the war machine for the north in motion. And Macintosh was part of that system.

McIntosh served with Rucker in the capital for the remainder of the Civil War, in the position as chief clerk. He was a handsome man, with dark eyes and the dark complexion of an aboriginal. And he was an excellent horseman. He would have made a mark in the Washington social circles and obviously caught the eye of Mary (Mollie) Garrett. More than a year after the end of the Civil War, on October 13, 1866, he and Mollie were married.[5]

Mollie was the eldest of three girls in the Garrett family of Baltimore, Maryland. The household included her mother and father, sisters Sally and Katherine, the black servant Mammy Lindy, and her "thieving son George." The family was fairly well-to-do; Katherine later described Mollie as being "brought up on family antique mahogany and rosewood and had studied her lessons at a table sacred to the card games of General Washington when he used to visit our ancestors...."[6]

Tallest of the three girls, Mollie held herself straight, her hair pulled softly back to rest in a small bun midway up the back of her head, framing a full-shaped face, and softened with curls at the forehead. She was considered a lively young woman whose temper could

Portrait of Lieutenant Donald McIntosh, 1873. McIntosh was born at Hudson's Bay post, Jasper House, in what is now Alberta.

flare up if challenged. For Mollie, music was a passion. Later a book written by Katherine's daughter, from Katherine's notes, painted a colourful, romantic picture of life in the west for Mollie and Donald. She described a meeting between husband and wife:

Courtesy of Glen Swanson.

Molly (Mary) McIntosh. Photo by E.E. Henry of Leavenworth, Kansas, probably taken while Lieutenant McIntosh was stationed in Kansas between August 1869 and April 1870.

Suddenly, from behind a wooden pillar, stepped the tall, lithe figure of an army officer in uniform, wearing a forage cap which bore the number 7, and a pair of shoulder straps showing the insignia of a first lieutenant.

"There's Donald," exclaimed Mollie as excitedly as though they had been separated a month.

He hurried toward us, and, as I looked into his strong, purposeful face and kindly, dark eyes, I suddenly knew that Mollie was a very lucky woman.... Donald smiled, and snow-white teeth flashed from behind his thin lips.[7]

But Mr. Garrett, Mollie's father, was not so enamoured of the young man. Katherine wrote, "I recalled the stormy scene when Mollie married Donald in deliberate defiance of our high-strung father, whose favourite slogan was, 'A word and a blow,' and who contended violently that the army and the plains were no fit setting for any man's daughter."[8]

While still in Washington, Donald McIntosh was commissioned second lieutenant in the Seventh Cavalry on August 17, 1867. He joined the regiment at Fort Harker, Kansas, on October 16 of that year, assigned to Company M. At that time, the Seventh was spread out in Kansas with units operating out of the camps on Big Creek, Fort Hays, Fort Wallace, Harker, Larned, Riley, Leavenworth, Dodge, and Zarah. A few of the men were at Camp Supply.

McIntosh was assigned to detached service in the spring of 1868 to serve as escort to a survey party at Plum Creek, Nebraska, for a month. He rejoined his company on June 5, and became ill on June 25, probably from dysentery. He would remain on the "sick list" for ten months, thus missing the upcoming Washita Campaign.

Another Canadian who was at the site of Custer's Last Stand in 1876 had first served in the Civil War. Born in Canada in 1837, place of birth not listed, James George MacAdams had joined the Sixth Kentucky Cavalry during the Civil War and was commissioned second lieutenant on February 28, 1863. He was mustered out as captain on September 6, 1865. Two years later MacAdams re-enlisted as second lieutenant in the Second Cavalry on March 7, 1867. He was promoted to first lieutenant on July 18, 1868. The Second Cavalry was later assigned to the Dakota Territory and became part of the Terry expedition eight years later.

CHAPTER 7

THE BATTLE OF WASHITA

T HE WASHITA RIVER FORMS IN THE TEXAS PANHANDLE AND runs parallel to, and just south of, the Canadian River in what is now Oklahoma, dipping southeast toward the Wichita Mountains. Red dust hills frame the north end of the river valley where Cheyenne Chief Black Kettle had chosen to settle a band of his people, including women and children. Reports on the numbers vary from 350 to 2,000 people. His village on the edge of the river included mostly Cheyenne, with some Arapaho, Kiowa, and Lakota.

It was about 100 miles south of the Kansas border. The village was in the heart of Indian Territory and sat 100 miles northwest of Fort Cobb. Chief Black Kettle understood it was where "friendly Indians" could and should be. He and Chief Big Mouth of the Arapahos had returned from Fort Cobb only a few days earlier. They had been seeking assurance from Colonel (Brevet Major-General) William Hazen, that their people would be safe. But it seemed their chances were slim since Hazen already had Natives from two Indian tribes camping at his fort, calling on him for food and protection.

Notes from the meeting of November 20, 1868, show that Black Kettle told Hazen that he didn't feel afraid to go among the white people:

> BLACK KETTLE, Cheyenne chief. ... The Cheyenne do not fight at all this side of the Arkansas [River]; they do not trouble Texas, but north of the Arkansas they are almost always at war. When lately north of

the Arkansas, some young Cheyennes were fired upon and then the fight began. I have always done my best to keep my young men quiet, but some will not listen, and since the fighting began I have not been able to keep them all at home. But we all want peace, and I would be glad to move all my people down this way; I could then keep them all quietly near camp. My camp is now on the Washita, 40 miles east of the Antelope Hills, and I have there about 180 lodges.

I speak only for my own people; I cannot speak nor control the Cheyennes north of the Arkansas.

BIG MOUTH, Arapaho chief. I have come down here, a long distance to this country in which I was born, to these prairies between the Wichita mountains and the mountains of the Arkansas, over which I roamed when a boy, to see all these Indians, my friends, and white men, who are my brothers, to have a talk. I look upon you [General Hazen] as the representative of the Great Father at Washington, and I came to you because I wish to do right; had I wished to do any wrong I never would have come near you....

GENERAL HAZEN.... I am sent here as a peace chief; all here is to be peace but north of the Arkansas is General Sheridan, the great war chief, and I do not control him; and he has all the soldiers who are fighting the Arapahoes and Cheyennes. Therefore, you must go back to your country, and if the soldiers come to fight, you must remember they are not from me, but from the great war chief, and with him you must make peace.... I cannot stop the war, but will send your talk to the great Father, and if he sends me orders to treat you like the friendly Indians I will send out to you to come in. But you must keep well out beyond the friendly Kiowas and Commanches. I am satisfied that you want peace; that it has not been you, but your bad men, that have made the war, and I will do all I can for you to bring peace; ...

Recorded by order of Colonel and Brevet Major General W.B. Hazen....[1]

There had been Indian raids on white settlements that year by young Cheyenne warriors, but Black Kettle had not taken part in them.

Several miles downstream from Chief Black Kettle's village other camps held between 6,000 and 8,000 men, women, and children, a mix of Cheyenne, Arapaho, and Kiowa.

Black Kettle had been a chief of the Council of Forty-Four for the past thirty-four years. And since the gold rush days began, he had recognized that the white man was taking over more and more of Indian land. In 1861 he signed a treaty to confine the Cheyenne to the Sand Creek reservation in southern Colorado. And in 1863 he and another chief travelled to Washington to see President Abraham Lincoln. This may have confirmed what he already had recognized — the size of the white population and that his people could not win an all-out war against it.

But tribal warriors didn't agree with the Fort Wise Treaty and launched major attacks on white settlements. Black Creek opposed this, but seems to have had to tolerate it. In 1864, under public pressure, the Colorado governor called in Colonel John Chivington to organize the 100 Day volunteers. They had decided to reinforce their militia by raising the Third Colorado Cavalry of these short-term volunteers. The volunteers signed up for 100 days, with the only purpose being to fight the Indians.

In August of that year Colonel Chivington was quoted as saying, "Kill and scalp all, little and big … nits make lice." In September all peaceful Indians were ordered to report to Fort Lyon. There, Major Scott Anthony told Black Kettle his people would be safe if he moved them to Sand Creek, forty miles from the fort. He presented a white flag to Black Kettle as a sign he would protect the Natives.

The raids by young Indian warriors escalated. One raid resulted in the murder of a family outside Denver. The whole territory was enraged by the sight of the mutilated bodies when they were brought into town.

Then on November 29, 1864, just two months after the Fort Lyon meeting sent the Indians to Sand Creek, the military attacked at dawn. Chivington's troops were joined by men from the Colorado First Regiment and troops from Fort Lyon, led by Major Antony. The battle at Sand Creek lasted eight hours. Black Kettle and about 500 others managed to escape. Black Kettle saved his wife, Medicine Woman Later, but she was badly injured. Of the 200 Natives killed, most were women and children.

Chief Black Kettle moved south to Indian Territory and, despite the massacre at Sand Creek, continued to work for peace. He asked his people not to retaliate for Sand Creek, but the Dog Soldiers continued their raids. The next year, in 1865, the Cheyenne chief signed the Little Arkansas Treaty, and in 1867 signed the Treaty of Medicine Lodge, promoting peace between Indians and white people. A congressional hearing in Washington later denounced Colonel Chivington. The seventy-two-day hearing labelled the episode "a massacre."

By 1868 Chief Black Kettle was fifty-five years old and his leadership was waning. He had instructed his people to live in peace with the white man, but that year a young Cheyenne, Roman Nose, led a series of attacks on farmers and settlers.

On November 22, 1868, Custer had moved out from Beaver Creek Indian Territory, one hundred miles south of Fort Dodge, Kansas. He had eleven companies, about 700 men, and thirty days' rations. At his side was Lieutenant Cooke. The second Canadian in the Seventh, Second Lieutenant Donald McIntosh of Company M, missed the mission; he was on sick leave. McIntosh had become seriously ill on June 25, possibly with dysentery, and was on the sick list for the next ten months, only rejoining his company in May of 1869 at Fort Larned.

Twenty-two-year-old Lieutenant Cooke had been with the Seventh Cavalry for two years now. He was, at times, regimental adjutant, and he had become part of Custer's close circle of friends. While on a campaign in search of hostile Indians near the Platte River in Kansas the previous year he had been involved in the troopers' desertion incident, and was a witness in the Custer court martial.

By 1868 the army's campaign against the Indians was in full force. General Philip H. Sheridan was commanding the Department of Missouri. His strategy was to attack the tribes of the Southern Plains in the winter when they would be least able to resist. He didn't differentiate between friendly Indians and the troublemakers. At the start of the 1868–69 campaign he wrote: "I am of the belief that these Indians require to be soundly whipped, and the ring-leaders in the present trouble hung, their ponies killed, and such destruction of the property as will make them very poor."

And he felt Custer was the man to carry out his strategy. He ordered Custer to hunt the Cheyennes who were thought to be responsible for the raids along the Saline and Solomon Rivers in Kansas. Custer was to find the winter hideouts of the hostile Indians who would not give up or come to the reservations peacefully. And he had orders to administer whatever punishments he was able to.

Custer had not always supported the idea of all-out war against the Natives. In a letter to his wife Elizabeth dated the previous year, May 2, 1867, from Fort Hays, Kansas, he wrote:

> I wrote a very strong letter recently *against* an Indian War, depicting as strongly as I could the

serious results that would follow ... putting a stop to trains on the Overland route, interfering with the work on the Pacific Railroad, all of which would be a national calamity. I regard the recent outrages (Indian attacks on white settlements) as the work of small groups of irresponsible young men, eager for war.

... Should a war be waged, none would be more determined than I to make it a war of extermination ... but I consider we are not yet justified in declaring such a war.[2]

But now it was on. Custer's planned route was across the Kansas border south to the Canadian River, down the river eastward to Fort Cobb, southeast toward the Washita (Wichita) Mountains, then northwest back to Beaver Creek. The mountains stretch in a west-east direction in what is now Oklahoma and Arkansas. The whole march was about 250 miles.

When the reveille was sounded at the Seventh Cavalry camp at four that morning the snow was already six inches deep and falling rapidly. Indian guides and scouts in the lead and the band at the head of the column, the troopers set out to the strains of "The Girl I Left Behind Me."

The second day on the trail they forded the icy Canadian River and Custer sent his second-in-command, Major Joel Elliott, down river with Indian scouts to reconnoitre. After a day and a half, word came back they'd spotted fresh tracks of a war-party, 150-strong, heading south.

Leaving eighty men to guard the wagons, Custer moved southeast, joining up with Elliott at sunset. Taking only time to eat, they moved into the valley of the Washita River. At ten o'clock that night they were still in the saddles. Custer moved forward just behind the scouts while the cavalry stayed about a half mile behind to avoid surprise by the Indians. Mile after mile, silently they moved — no whisper, no matches, no pipes. The Indian scouts halted, reporting the smell of fire. They said a village was two or three miles ahead.

The command resumed the march, and at the crest of a hill one of the Indian scouts peered into the valley and pointed out the Indian village below. Custer dismounted and moved up. He heard dogs and the sound of an infant's cry.

It was now after midnight. Custer ordered his officers to remove their sabres so the clank of metal would not be heard. He divided the cavalry into four detachments. One would move to the woods below the village, another down river to the woods there, the third to the crest of a hill north of the village.

> Major Elliott commanded the column of Companies G, H, and M to the left, almost at the rear of the village; Colonel Thompson commanded the one consisting of B and F troops, which moved in a corresponding manner from our right to a position which was to connect with that of Major Elliot, Colonel Meyers commanded the third column, composed of E and I troops, which was to take position in the valley and timber a little less than a mile to my right.[3]

The fourth detachment, Companies A, C, D, and K, Custer's own, remained where it was. Custer considered Lieutenant Cooke the best shot in the regiment. He put him in command of a detachment of forty sharpshooters. He lined up a squadron on the left and one on the right. And Cooke, with his forty sharpshooters, formed up in advance of the left squadron, which was on foot.

> Fortunately, in my command were a considerable number of young officers, nearly all of whom were

full of soldierly ambition and eager to grasp any opportunity which opened the way to honorable preferment. The difficulty was not in finding an officer properly qualified in every way to command the sharpshooters, but ... to designate a leader par excellence. The choice fell upon Colonel [*sic*] Cooke ...[4]

The attacks would be timed, as everything depended on the simultaneous timing and the element of surprise. This meant the "home" detachment, Custer's, would wait in position for four hours. The troopers dismounted, but even foot stamping and pacing were prohibited in case of noise. The soldiers stood or lay on the frozen ground holding their horses' reins. When the moon had gone down and the time approached, they discarded their overcoats and haversacks, anything that would impede their action in the fight. They moved down to the valley.

The moon had gone down; the night was black. It had snowed all night, more than a foot, and it was bitter cold. The men stood beside their horses unable to stomp their feet to keep warm for fear of alerting the enemy. A rifle shot cracked from the far side of the village. Custer, astride his white horse, gave the word. The cornet player gave the sign, and the band broke into "Garry Owen," the regimental tune. The Seventh Cavalry of the United States Army rushed into action from all four sides of the village. The Battle of Washita began.

Lieutenant-Colonel George Armstrong Custer headed his first major attack in the army's "Indian Wars" on November 27, 1868.

The rifle shot cracked from the far side of the village, launching the attack. Custer led the largest battalion into the village then watched from a knoll to the south as his soldiers drove the Cheyenne from their lodges, half-dressed and running in all directions.

Chief Black Kettle was known to fly the stars and stripes on his teepee as a sign of peace. Some reports say he came forward to meet the soldiers, even hoisting a white flag. Whatever the truth, Chief

Black Kettle and his wife Medicine Woman Later were killed while trying to cross the Washita River. One of Custer's Indian guides took the chief's scalp. Black Kettle's fourteen-year old son shot the horse out from under Captain Beneteen, who later shot the boy.

The battle lasted about two hours. The cavalry took the village and set up a makeshift hospital there. Many of the officers fell. Colonel Barnitz was wounded and sent to the hospital. There was no word from Major Elliott. And the army was now surrounded. Mounted warriors in full regalia came in from surrounding encampments:

Courtesy of Denver Public Library, Western History Collection, x32364.

Cheyenne Chief Black Kettle, seated extreme left, with a group of Native men, representing the Cheyenne, Arapahoe, Sioux, and Kiowa people.

Cheyennes, Arapahoes, Kiowas. Despite this, the supply wagons managed to get ammunition through to the cavalry.

The troops destroyed more than fifty lodges in the village: forty-seven belonged to the Cheyenne, two to the Arapahoe, and two to the Sioux. They destroyed 500 buffalo robes and the village's winter supply of dried buffalo meat.

In his notes Custer tells how he dealt with the 870 Indian ponies, now in his possession, which he knew the Native warriors would follow and try to recover:

> This, with sixty prisoners to convey, our own wounded to care for, the exhausted condition of our troops, might have resulted in the loss of all we had gained. Having caused the best ponies to be selected for our captives, I issued an order as painful to decide on as to carry out — that the unwanted ponies should be shot.
>
> The sad side of the story is the killed and wounded. Captain Hamilton ... Major Elliott who with 15 men charged after a small band of Indians and pursued them too far ... nineteen enlisted men ... three officers and eleven enlisted men wounded....[5]

The figure for the death toll among the Native people varies. Some say a total of fifty, others say about seventy — twenty warriors and fifty women and children. Custer then rounded up the sixty prisoners — women, children, old men, and a few warriors — that he took back to camp with him. He later wrote that "... in the excitement of the fight as well as in self-defense, it so happened that some of the squaws and a few children were killed and wounded."

Around three in the afternoon Custer decided to take the offensive. What he needed was something to divert the Indians still waiting to make their next move. He made his decision. With band playing and colours flying, Custer marched down river as if leaving in that direction. After dark that night he retraced his steps, camping after midnight in the valley of the Washita. The men built bonfires to warm themselves as the Indians had made off with their discarded overcoats.

The next day they met the supply wagons and returned to Camp Supply about thirty miles south of the Kansas border. Approaching camp, his Indian scouts celebrated the victory by yelling, firing their rifles, and hanging on the sides and necks of their horses while galloping at high speed. Next came the band playing, then the troopers. Cooke's sharpshooters were given place of honour near the front as they paraded before General Sheridan.

Captain Louis Hamilton was the grandson of a former secretary of the treasury in Washington and one of the youngest captains in the army. He had been shot through the heart as his unit charged through the village. Willie Cooke was asked to join Custer and Sheridan as a pall bearer at Captain Hamilton's funeral, another indication of his position in the Custer circle.

The bodies of Major Elliott and his party of fifteen soldiers were discovered weeks later. There was criticism that Custer had not sent help out for Elliott at the time. Custer's answer was that in the midst of battle it was not known that any detachment had gone off on an independent chase.

Although controversy swirled around the results of the Seventh Cavalry's operation in Indian Territory, both because of the army losses and the Indian massacre, General Sheridan stood behind the mission. He showed his approval in a message to Custer:

> ... and the Major-General Commanding [Sheridan] expresses his thanks to the officers and men engaged in the Battle of Washita, and his special congratulations to their distinguished commander Brevet

Major-General George A. Custer for the efficient and gallant service opening the campaign against the hostile Indians north of the Arkansas.[6]

CHAPTER 8

THE AFTERMATH

A S SETTLERS MOVED WESTWARD, THE CLASHES WITH THE
Natives and raids on outposts became more and more common, and the government became more and more determined to
overcome the Indians. Not long before, the federal Indian Bureau
had been handed over to the War Department and the brutal Battle
of Washita was an example of the army's determination to demoral-
ize the Indians, hostile or not, and bring them in to the reservations
where they could be controlled.

Two sides quickly built up in the wave of controversy swirling
around the battle. There were those who backed the strong punitive
policy of the army; the army blamed the "Indian rings" or bands of
young Indian soldiers as did many of the Indians themselves. But
for the military it was as if anyone disagreeing with their concept
of harsh treatment, even extermination, of the Plains tribes, was
against progress. On the other side were the advocates of a "peace
policy." Many of these were Indian agents who worked directly with
the various chiefs and Indian bands.

In Washington both factions were having their say. In a resolution reached on December 18, 1868, less than a month after the
Battle of Washita, the Senate asked the Secretary of Interior to
send the Senate any information it had in relation to the hostile or
peaceful character of the Indians recently killed or captured by the
United States troops under the command of Custer. The resolution
also wanted the department of the Interior "to inform the Senate
whether said Indians were, at the time of said conflict, residing on

the reservation assigned them under treaty stipulations; and if so, whether they had taken up said residence in pursuance of instructions emanating from the department of the Interior."

The resolution was an opening for the anti-army forces, but for some reason they didn't come forward in full force. There were no full-blown complaints from the anti-army forces.

But in the Indian Territory of the west, one Indian agent in particular felt the blow of the Battle of Washita. Major E.W. Wynkoop, Cheyenne tribal agent, had been outraged at the massacre of Sand Creek a few years previous; the massacre at Black Kettle's village hit him hard. Major Wynkoop wrote to N.G. Taylor, commissioner of Indian Affairs in Washington, expressing his dismay at the army's campaign against the Indians. He said he had gathered 500 friendly Cheyenne together assuring them the protection of the United States. "They were then attacked by volunteer troops from Colorado, nearly 200 women and children and old men brutally murdered."

EN ROUTE TO FORT COBB, November 29 (1868).

... The infamous massacre at Sand Creek will not soon be forgotten. The Indians were naturally under the impression that I was responsible for the outrage; but after they fully understood my position, I became, at their request, their agent, and they have renewed the confidence they had in me previous to the Sand Creek murder, trusting me implicitly up to the time of General Hancock's memorable expedition, they then having received assurance from me that General Hancock would not harm them, and seeing me with him, whom I had been induced to accompany under assurances from himself that his mission was a peaceful one.

Upon the destruction of their lodges and other property, again they naturally inferred the fault was mine, and some time since, while in the performance of my duty among the Indians I came near losing my life in consequence; but I again succeeded in retaining their confidence, and am now under orders to proceed to Fort Cobb, on the Washita River, and congregate what Indians I can of my agency at that point or vicinity....

Wynkoop realized volunteer troops along with other Indian tribe members, enemies of the Plains Indians, were heading that way, and he refused to gather the Cheyennes of his agency at a point where those troops would arrive.

They [Cheyenne] will readily respond to my call but I most certainly refuse to again be the instrument of the murder of innocent women and children.... All left me under the circumstances, with the present state of feelings I have in this matter, is now to respectfully tender my resignation and return the commission which I have so far earnestly endeavored to fulfill the requirements of....[1]

Major-General Philip Sheridan was in the field, at the depot on the North Canadian River, at the junction of Beaver Creek. A few years earlier the government had broken up its western army into various sectors, one being the division of Missouri. Sheridan added his reaction to the Battle of Washita in a letter to Brevet Major-General W.A. Nichols, assistant adjutant general, military division of the Missouri at St. Louis, Missouri, dated December 2, 1868. Sheridan reported the arrival of the Seventh Cavalry, with fifty-seven Indian women and a number of small children as prisoners:

The victory was complete, and the punishment
just. The trail of the party which led General Custer
to the Indian camp was that of a party returning
with the scalps of three white men. Among them
was that of our courier, killed between Dodge and
Larned, and the mail he was carrying was found in
the Indian camp; also the mules of Clark's train;
also photographs and other articles taken from
houses robbed on the Saline and Solomon [rivers].

.... Flour, sugar, and coffee, found in Black
Kettle's village, was furnished by General Hazen.
Something should be done to stop this anomaly.
I am ordered to fight these Indians, and General
Hazen is permitted to feed them. All the Arapahoes
[sic] were in the vicinity of the fight, and took part
in it, and the women prisoners tell me that most
of the depredations along the line of the Arkansas
were committed by them; still they are now having
flour, sugar, and coffee issued to them, even to war
parties going out to depredate and kill.

I simply wish to call the attention of the
Lieutenant General [Sherman] to this complicated
condition of affairs, so that he may at once see all
the evils resulting from it.[2]

But the superintendent of Indian Affairs, Thomas Murphy,
castigated the army for the attack. Murphy wrote to Indian Affairs
commissioner Taylor from Atchison, Kansas, that he was "sick
at heart" when he read General Sheridan's report of the Battle of
Washita. The letter is dated December 4, 1868. Murphy said Chief
Black Kettle was one of the "truest friends the whites ever had
among the Indians of the plains":

He who, in 1864, purchased with his own ponies the white women and children captured on the Blue and Platte Rivers by the Dog Soldiers of the Cheyennes and by the Sioux, and freely delivered them up at Denver city to Colonel Chivington, who was at the time the military commandant of that place. After this he [Black Kettle] was induced, under promises of protection for his people, to bring them into the vicinity of Fort Lyon, where they were soon afterward pounced upon by the military, led by Chivington, and cruelly and indiscriminately murdered....

Black Kettle faced a great deal of criticism from his own people for the Sand Creek Massacre because he had led his people to the area when promised protection — protection that didn't materialize. Murphy outlined a number of times that Black Kettle urged his people to cooperate with the army. Murphy said it was the memory of the massacre of Sand Creek that drove Black Kettle to take his people south toward Fort Cobb. He noted that Sartau-ta, a powerful Kiowa chief who had been a strong proponent of peace over the past three years, had only broken that peace when he had been drawn into the Battle of Washita because he rushed to the support of Black Kettle.

Murphy warned that since this happened in the vicinity of Fort Cobb it would discourage other Indian tribes from settling peacefully near the fort.

And will have the effect of frightening away all those Indians who were expected to congregate in the vicinity of Fort Cobb, and of starting upon the war path many Indians who have been friendly disposed toward the government, thus costing the nation many valuable lives and millions of treasure....[3]

Lieutenant-General W.T. Sherman added his voice in a letter to three generals, Sheridan, Hazen, and Brevet General B.H. Grierson, dated December 23, 1868, from his headquarters at the military division of the Missouri at St. Louis, Missouri. He had sent copies of the generals' reports on the Battle of Washita to the War Department to counteract the insistence by Indian Affairs that Black Kettle's camp was friendly and Custer's battle was a second Sand Creek affair. He also called the press to account for what he called a misrepresentation of the story:

Our people cannot be humbugged into the belief that Black Kettle's camp was friendly, with its captive women and children, its herds of stolen horses, its stolen mail, arms, powder &c., trophies of war. I am well satisfied with Custer's attack, and would not have wept if he could have served Satanta's and Bull Bear's bands in the same style. I want you all to go ahead, kill and punish the hostile, rescue the captive white women and children, capture and destroy the ponies, lances, carbines, &c., of the Cheyennes, Araphoes, and Kiowas. Mark out the spots where they must stay, a view to economical support, until we can try and get them to be self-supporting, like the Cherokees and Choctaws.... If the game of the Indian Territory do not suffice for their support, the United States must feed them till they can raise tame cattle, sheep and hogs, and until they can raise patches of corn, potatoes, pumpkins, &c.

... The course I have indicated must be followed before Indian agents can pretend to manage the four bands now so construed to be at war, viz: Cheyennes, Araphahoes, Kiowas and Comanches.... I would like that Bull Bear and

Satanta should be killed before the tribes are allowed any favors at our hands.[4]

Early in the new year, on January 30, 1869, Secretary of the Interior O.H. Browning, replied to the Senate. It was only a short memorandum from N.G. Taylor, commissioner of Indian Affairs, dated the day before. The Office of Indian Affairs reported that "all the information this office has" regarding the Battle of Washita were two personal letters that Commissioner Taylor had received. There was one from J.S. Morrison, a former Indian Agency employee and scout in the Sheridan-Custer Indian campaign. The other was from Major E.W. Wynkoop, a former Cheyenne tribal agent.

The Morrison letter was really a letter from him to Indian agent Wynkoop seeking a job, but he did give some insight into the Washita affair. It was datelined Fort Dodge, Kansas, December 14, 1868. After a brief opening he refers to Washita:

John Smith, John Poysell and Jack Fitzpatrick have got in today. John S. was not in the fight (Battle of Washita) but John P. and Jack were. They all agree in stating that the official reports of the fight were very much exagerated [sic] that there was not over twenty Bucks killed, the rest, about forty, were women and children. The prisoners have got in today. They consisted of 53 women and children. One boy is Arapahoe. The rest are all Cheyennes. Mrs. Crocker is amongst them. She is badly wounded. She says that her child is killed. The women say that Black Kettle is killed.

The prisoners will be taken to Fort Riley. It is possible that I will be sent in charge of them. Genls. Sheridan and Custer have started on a new expedition. The officers say that he is going direct to Fort

Cobb, swearing vengenance [sic] on INDIANS
AND INDIAN AGENTS INDISCRIMINATELY.
When John's wife [a Cheyenne] heard of the fight
she tried to kill herself, first with a knife and next
with strychnine but Dr. Howard cured her from the
effects of it....[5]

Edward Wanshaer Wynkoop had a colourful career. On June 19,
1836, he was born into a wealthy Pennsylvania family, the youngest
son of John Wanshaer Wynkoop of Pennsylvania. He had travelled
west to Kansas and then farther west in the search of gold. For a while
he was sheriff of Arapaho County, Kansas territory. He signed up as
second lieutenant in the First Colorado Volunteers during the Civil
War, promoted to major after beating off a bid by Texans to capture
New Mexico and Colorado. Wynkoop had served under Major, later
Colonel, John Chivington.

He then was appointed United States Indian agent. As agent
to the Cheyenne and Arapaho he was a controversial figure for his

*Major Edward W. Wynkoop, kneeling front left, and Chief Black Kettle, seated
centre middle row, at Camp Weld Council, Denver, Colorado, September 1864.*

stand on their rights. He worked hard to prevent hostilities. He was a champion of the Native tribes under his authority. He blamed Congress for failing to appropriate funds for food and for withholding annuity payments.

In 1864, Wynkoop had met with Black Kettle and rescued four white children who were hostages of Cheyenne Dog Soldiers and made an unofficial peace accord with Black Kettle. It was Wynkoop who came to an agreement with the Cheyenne and the Arapaho to camp on Big Sandy River, Colorado, under the American flag and the white flag of peace.

Days later, on November 29, 1864, Colonel Chivington and soldiers from Fort Lyon attacked Sand Creek and the Indians who had surrendered under the Camp Weld Council, massacring hundreds. Wynkoop went head to head with Chivington over this. The government in Washington condemned Chivington and appointed Wynkoop to the War Department as brevet lieutenant-colonel, and agent for the Cheyenne and Arapaho.

It was difficult for him as Indian agent to regain the Indians' confidence — Bull Bear vowed to kill him and the Dog Soldiers wouldn't relent in their revenge.

By 1868, Wynkoop had had enough and resigned his post in protest over the army's aggressive new Indian policy. He said he refused to be party to "the murder of innocent women and children." He denounced the attack on Black Creek's village, comparing Custer to Chivington, and Washita to Sand Creek.

In a letter to Commissioner Taylor, Major Wynkoop wrote:

Philadelphia, January 26, 1869

Sir: In reply to your request to be furnished with all the information I have received relative to the battle of the Washita, I have the honor to state that all the information I have in regard to that affair has been gleaned from the public reports of the same, and in two letters I have received from Mr. James S. Morrison, who was formerly in the employ of my agency; one of his letters I herewith enclose, the other is in the possession of Colonel T. Tappan, of the Indian peace commission.

I am perfectly satisfied, however, that the position of Black Kettle and his immediate relations at the time of the attack upon their village was not a hostile one. I know that Black Kettle had proceeded to the point at which he was killed with the understanding that it was the locality where all those Indians who were friendly disposed should assemble; I know that such information has been conveyed to Black Kettle as the orders of the military authorities, and that he was also instructed that Fort Cobb was the point that the friendly Indians would receive subsistence at; and it is admitted by General Hazen, who is stationed at Fort Cobb, that Black Kettle had been to his headquarters a few days previous to his death. In regard to the charge that Black Kettle engaged in the depredations committed on the Saline River during the summer of 1868, I know the same to be utterly false, as Black Kettle at the time was camped near my agency on the Pawnee Fork. The said depredations were undoubtedly committed by a party of Cheyenne Indians but that same party proceeded with the Sioux Indians north from that point, and up to the time of Black Kettle's death had not returned to the Arkansas River. They have been Indians deserving of punishment, but unfortunately, they have not been those who received it at the hands of the troops at the battle of the Washita.

Black Kettle's village at the time of the attack upon it was situated upwards of 150-miles from any travelled road, in the heart of the Indian country. The military reports state that the ground was covered with snow and weather intensely cold. It is well known that the major portion of the village consisted of women and children, and yet the military reports are that they were engaged in hostilities, and excuse the attack for the reason that evidence was found in the camp that the said Indians were engaged in hostilities. How did they know that those evidences existed previous to the attack? Mr. Morrison states that there were 40 women and children killed. That fact needs no comment; it speaks for itself. I do not know whether the government desires to look at this office in a humane light or not, and if it desires to know whether it was right or wrong to attack the village referred to, I must emphatically pronounce it wrong and disgraceful.

With much respect, your obedient servant,

E. Wynkoop
Late United States Indian Agent[6]

By April of 1869 General Sheridan was in Chicago and offering Custer some leave time.

I am very much rejoiced at the success of your expedition, and feel very proud of our winter operations, and of the officers and men who bore privations so manfully.

I presume you will want a leave, and so spoke
to Genl. Schofield (Secretary of War) and, if you
desire such, you can have as long as you please.[7]

The Seventh Cavalry Regiment went home, home being the summer camp on Big Creek, just below Fort Hays, Kansas. Big Creek was also known as Camp Sturgis. The Canadians, Cooke and McIntosh, were at Sturgis. McIntosh and his wife Mollie had a tent a few tents down from Custer and his wife Libbie. In fact, they posed for photos in front of the tent with the Custers. And it was at this camp that McIntosh was promoted to first lieutenant in March of 1870.

Custer took leave in 1869, visiting Sheridan in Chicago then going on to Monroe, Michigan.

CHAPTER 9

COOKE AND CUSTER

W ILLIAM "WILLIE" COOKE ALSO TOOK LEAVE IN 1869. HE
rode the Atlantic Express back to Hamilton, Upper Canada,
the town he'd left seven years earlier. His life had changed signifi-
cantly during that period: he'd been on a tour of duty in the American
Civil War, and he'd seen the beginning of the Indian Wars.

Cooke stepped down from the train at the Great Western
Railway Station. With him were two guests, Lieutenant-Colonel,
Brevet Major-General, George Armstrong Custer and former Detroit
mayor, Kirkland C. Barker.

The Great Western had arrived in Hamilton fifteen years earlier with all the pomp and display worthy of such an historical
event. At two o'clock in the morning of January 18, 1854, a wood-
burning steam engine pulled the first train into the town. The large,
welcoming crowd had been celebrating all night. The Rochester
Brass Band that had travelled across the border from New York
State played "Yankee Doodle" and "Long Live the Queen." The
train didn't leave for Detroit until four hours later. By the time
Cooke and his party arrived in 1869, the original small wooden
station with two-storey tower had been gusssied up with stucco to
resemble stone.

In the 1860s Hamilton, at the western end of Lake Ontario, was a
commercial city with a population of more than 10,000. The city was
the headquarters for the Great Western, and had become a railway
hub for immigrants heading from New York to the American mid-
west, and for western crops heading to the Hamilton port.

Cooke had a prominent branch of his family in Hamilton. His grandfather, John Winer, had moved to the city from Durham, New York, years earlier. Winer established a wholesale drug firm that became the National Drug Company at 56 King Street East. He also served for a time as a city councillor.

John Winer had opened his first drug store in 1830. By 1845 he was manufacturing a wide range of medicines, including "Universal Family Ointment for the cure of Pains in the Bones, Gout, Scurvy, Boils, Itch, Cancers and Burns." He sold them retail and wholesale. That same year his store was destroyed by fire but Winer rebuilt at No. 3 Stinson's Block on King Street East. By the time his grandson and Custer visited, Winer had formed a partnership and begun selling druggist supplies on a wholesale basis only. His business interests also included a partnership in the Hamilton Glass Works that produced various types of bottles, preserving jars, and insulators for telegraph lines.

Cooke's grandfather was also active in city politics. For eight years he was chairman of the Board of Police, which was the city's governing body after the legislature named it a Police Village in 1833. And Winer was one of Hamilton's pioneer aldermen, sitting on city council for many years.

None of this would have been lost on Custer. Such a successful and prominent businessman would appeal to Custer, as did the prominent men of New York City when he visited there. He would also be aware of the family connection, through Cooke's mother, with President Andrew Johnson.

Cooke's grandfather, John Winer, met his guests at the station and took them to the family home at 96 Main Street East. Custer seemed pleased enough with the reception and attention that he stayed at the Winer home for several days.

Cooke was a Custer favourite, and was well-liked by his commanding officer. Cooke was so well trusted that it was said he was also responsible for Elizabeth "Libbie" Custer's welfare. If capture by the Indians was imminent, Cooke was to shoot her. This was the blanket instruction to all the officers who might have Custer's wife in their care.

Cooke was considered loyal, obedient, and a social charmer. Single officers at the forts and posts in the mid-west depended on visits by officers' wives' friends, single women, for social companionship. Libbie Custer did her part in bringing friends out from Michigan to the various posts she and her husband were at, and Cooke was connected to a few of them. He and Tom Custer are often quoted as being partial to the Wadsworth girls, Emma and Nellie Wadsworth. There's a photo of the four of them together.

But the more serious romance was with Anna Darragh, more often referred to as Diana. She spent some time with the Seventh Cavalry in the first year of its operation. She is described as "a Michigan grocer's daughter who liked to go adventuring."[1] Diana Darragh was from Monroe, Michigan, and in her early twenties she ventured west. While not as wealthy as Cooke's family, her father Lewis Darrah was an important businessman in Monroe and the family was socially prominent. Libbie Custer and Diana were childhood friends and classmates at the young Ladies Seminary and Collegiate Institute in Monroe. Diana was a bridesmaid at the Custer wedding. She was called by various affectionate names, but usually Diana or Anna. In the mid 1850s the expectation for women of that rank and age was to be successfully married, but for Diana even a pretty face didn't seem to work. At one time she had been engaged to a member of the Seventh Cavalry, Lieutenant Myles Moylan, but that had broken off. In 1864, just past her twentieth birthday, she wrote to her newly married friend Libbie Custer: "I imagine your loving partiality induces you to think that gentlemen you know would fancy me, but to be, as you say, practical what am I to do for somebody to love me? I despair."[2]

Libbie invited Diana to Kansas when the Seventh was being formed. She was with the Custers at Fort Leavenworth, and she and

Cooke were the Custers' guests on New Year's Day 1868. In 1869, when Cooke and Custer stopped in Monroe on their way to Hamilton, Willie Cooke spent time with Diana again, his visit reported to have gone far into the early morning hours.

Custer was unhappy with the whole affair, whether that was from real concern or not wanting to lose control over his close friend. He had Mollie McIntosh, wife of "Tosh" McIntosh, spread gossip about Moylan's former fiancée. It seems Diana Darragh spent more time than was acceptable pursuing officers and became the object of gossip and criticism. There were rumours she had broken an engagement to another officer, rumours she may have been a kleptomaniac and that's why she was sent west in the first place.

> It was the beautiful Anna Darragh who was found to be a kleptomaniac during K's girlhood and who followed her fiancé out west to his army post after her disgrace. She afterwards claimed to be married to this young man — Captain Norville of General Custer's staff. But when the Captain died his obituary said "he never married."[3]

Her father was a Justice of the Peace, and this could have played a role in keeping this secret. At any rate there was no more reference to Diana in Willie Cooke's life.

During 1869, Cooke had served as Custer's aide-de-camp for a month and a half, had been transferred around to command different companies of the Seventh, and was granted leave on December 3. He had that extended for three months. Cooke returned to the regiment March 22, 1870.

Custer was on the move that year, travelling without his wife Libbie, who stayed at Fort Leavenworth, but writing detailed letters, many telling of the grand reception he received in society. In a letter to his wife he noted his pledge to himself to never again play cards or games of chance for money, while a married man. There were charges of drunkenness, cowardice, and sex offenses against the Seventh Cavalry.[4] Reports suggested Cooke and other officers were treated for venereal disease.

In July, Custer travelled to New York City on business and pleasure, again without Libbie. He was feeling the effects of what he considered a backwater posting in the mid-west and was looking for career opportunities, but he was also enjoying the social scene.

He wrote to his wife just after arriving in New York City, a letter that exemplified how much he enjoyed his celebrity, and the ladies:

> Within an hour I had received more invitations than I can accept....
>
> ... A friend has taken a box at the Academy of Music for ten nights, paying for it $120. He invited me to occupy a seat in it whenever I choose. Miss Kellogg also expects me behind the scenes.
>
> Is it not strange to think of me meeting to confer with such men as Belmont, Astor, Travers, Barkers, Morton and Bliss?
>
> Genl. Young would like to have us stationed at Atlanta. Is it not nice to have prominent Southern people desire to have us with them?[5]

By the end of the year he was staying with General Sheridan in Chicago.

There was no sign of a promotion and some indication the Seventh Cavalry might be broken up, so Custer was unsure of his future in the army. In March 1871, he was posted to Elizabethtown, Kentucky, for what became a two-year stay.

While at Elizabethtown, Custer worked on his book, *My Life on the Plains*, telling his side of the story over the last few years. The editor of a 1952 edition, Milo Milton Quaife, says Custer had not really learned how to fight Indian Wars, but he eventually acquired a reputation as the country's best Indian fighter. "His undoubted brilliance was marred, however by certain defects of character which caused him infinite trouble to the end of his life."[6]

In his book, Custer defended his actions, both regarding the 1867 fiasco that led to his court martial, and the circumstances surrounding the Battle of Washita. What editor Milo Milton Quaife called

> his headlong retreat before an enemy only intent upon fleeing in the opposite direction seems to indicate that for perhaps the only time in his career he had lost his nerve. That he greatly exaggerated the opposition made by the warriors from the lower villages is testified by Lieutenant Godfrey and by the obvious facts disclosed in large part in his own narrative.[7]

Quaife says the most serious blot on Custer's entire career on the plains was the indifference he displayed at the Battle of Washita to the fate of Major Elliot's detachment.

> Custer's own narrative discloses that the "most thorough search" he caused to be made for Ellliot's men was limited to the immediate vicinity of the captured village; and the fact that their mangled corpses, conspicuous in their snowy background, were lying only two miles away exposes the "thoroughness" of the search that was made.[8]

Custer's writings were carried as essays in the magazine *The Galaxy* and later published as a book. In it Custer revealed just how close he was with Lieutenant Cooke, whom he referred to by his brevet rank as Colonel Cooke. Cooke led the sharpshooters and

Custer depended on him to lead various forays into Indian country. At one point when Cooke, with a dozen men, was bringing supplies to Custer and some of the troops, he did not find them at the designated spot. Custer had moved on. Cooke, with only a small party, and in hostile country, made camp in a stand of timber.

> Fear, or a lack of the highest order of personal courage, was not numbered among the traits of character possessed by this officer. After seeing that the animals were properly secured for the night, and his men made comfortable, he sat down by the camp fire awaiting preparation of his evening meal.[9]

In Custer's telling, Cooke viewed his situation much as the massacred Kidder party, which had had the identical number of troopers, twelve, was separated from his cavalry, and could possibly share the same fate. Although Custer's scout, California Joe, did find him, the very next day Cooke spotted a mass of Indians approaching from the distance causing further concern. Custer quotes both Cooke and California Joe:

> "Well, Joe, we must do the best we can; there is no use in running."
> "You're right," replied Joe, "an Injun'll beat a white man runnin' every time, so I 'spect our best holt is fitin', but, Lor' a' mercy! Look at 'em; thar ain't enuff uv us to go half round!"[10]

The worries were needless since it was an Arapahoe chief, Yellow Bear, and his party — Indians who had made peace with the United States government.

Cooke was also his close companion as Custer pushed ahead of the expedition into what is now the Texas Panhandle to meet with

Cheyenne chiefs at a spot on the tributary of the Red River, not far south of the Canadian River, in what is now Oklahoma. As Custer told it, he sat with the chiefs, smoking the peace pipe in Medicine Arrow's tent. It's not clear if McIntosh's company was part of that forward detachment, but all the while Custer smoked the peace pipe, Cooke was in a nearby tent hoping all was going well.

One of the objects of the expedition was to obtain the release of two white girls who were being held by the Indians. Just when Custer was ready to set out, a young man named Brewster had approached him with the story of his sister, Mrs. Morgan. Her husband had been shot down by the Indians four months previous. He had survived, although badly injured, but his nineteen-year-old wife had been taken. Brewster had no idea where she was. Custer allowed him to join the mission.

The troops made camp, and a number of chiefs assembled around the campfire. Custer organized the capture of four chiefs and warriors as a bargaining tool to obtain the girls' release. He also demanded the Cheyenne abandon the war path and return to the reservation, relocate the village near Fort Supply, and report to the military commander there.

Negotiations continued a number of days with Custer holding three of the chiefs. He finally gave them a last chance or else the chiefs would be killed and the village attacked. Just at sundown, twenty mounted Indians were seen approaching the military camp. The two girls were on one pony in the lead.

If the three chiefs thought they were home free, they hadn't counted on the strength of the government's determination to control the Indians — or Custer's cunning. Custer quickly pointed out that the hostages, the three chiefs, wouldn't be returned until the other conditions were met: the Cheyenne abandoning the warpath, returning to the reservation, and reporting to the military commander at Camp Supply. Custer marched back to Camp Supply with his hostages.[11]

Quaife calls settling the issue with the Cheyenne without bloodshed Custer's biggest victory.

Custer's last campaign on the Southern Plains ...
was a remarkable performance which deserves far
greater renown than has ever been accorded it. In its
conduct he displayed a complete mastery of Indian
psychology and of the art of frontier warfare.[12]

Custer went on to Fort Hays with his hostages. Within a short time, two of the three chiefs had been killed by their jailers — an incident Custer called a misunderstanding. Soon the other Arapahoe chiefs came for their chiefs. The remaining chief, Red Nose, and the hostages from the Battle of Washita, were released to the fate of the American Indian, the reservation at Camp Supply.

CHAPTER 10

THE SEVENTH CAVALRY HEADS SOUTH

ALTHOUGH WILLIE COOKE IS MOSTLY REFERRED TO AS AN adjutant, he did spend some time on active duty with regimental companies. In other words, he wasn't strictly a desk soldier, as is sometimes claimed.[1]

In 1867, at age twenty, he was assigned to Company H and continued with that company on and off throughout that year and into the next. On November 10, 1868, he took up special duty as commanding officer of the sharpshooters for the Battle of Washita. Early in the next year he was on detached service scouting the Red River. For a short time he was Custer's aide-de-camp then returned to his company on March 24. In April he was transferred to Company I, at times in command of the company. He was relieved of that command in December and granted a three-month leave, returning to the regiment March 22, 1870, at Fort Leavenworth, Kansas, where he spent some time as post adjutant.

During the Civil War, Taylor Barracks in Louisville, Kentucky, named for former president Zachary Taylor, had been a military induction centre for African-American soldiers. The wooden barracks sat on the southern outskirts of Louisville, not far from Beargrass Creek. The wooden frame buildings were arranged in a square, and eventually grew to cover four blocks. The post included a jail, hospital, and reception hall. There were officers' quarters, quartermaster storehouses, and workshops. After the war the army kept the barracks open as a base for both white and black soldiers.

When the Seventh Cavalry was assigned to reconstruction duty in the south (reconstruction of the country after the Civil War), the regimental headquarters were established in Louisville. Cooke moved to Taylor Barracks as the regimental adjutant on July 1, 1871. As adjutant it was his job to assist the garrison commanding officer; he was back in an administrative position again.

Cooke took a number of leave breaks throughout 1872. On March 13, 1873, he moved north as the Seventh Cavalry prepared for its task in North Dakota Territory. He took up duties with the Seventh headquarters in St. Paul, Minnesota, in May.

Cooke seemed to take leave whenever he could or wanted. He was on leave in June, returning only to go off again on July 21 for seven days, extended to six months "with permission to cross the seas." This had not been an automatic permission. General Sheridan originally denied the request. Cooke wrote to General William Tecumseh Sherman and got the permission he sought.[2]

At Big Creek in Kansas, also known as Camp Sturgis, Donald McIntosh and his wife had a tent just a few tents down from Custer and his wife Libbie. Mollie and Donald became part of the coterie of officers and wives surrounding the Custers. An 1869 photo at Big Creek shows the McIntoshes posed with the Custers and others under an open seating-tent.

It was at Big Creek that McIntosh was promoted to first lieutenant in August of 1869, effective March 22, 1870. He was assigned to Company G.

With McIntosh's promotion to first lieutenant came an incident that threw a black cloud over his military career, at least temporarily. Seven days after his promotion he was arrested by the new commanding officer, Colonel Samuel D. Sturgis, who had replaced Smith. Colonel Sturgis, who had taken a dislike to the young officer, advised the board of review in Washington that he be dismissed. Sturgis wrote of Donald McIntosh:

Eminently inefficient through ... extreme indifference to his official duties, giving him the appearance of desiring to render the smallest possible service compatible with absolute security of his commission. If he were an enlisted man he would pass as a malingerer.[3]

While awaiting his hearing before the Board of Review, known as the Benzine Board, McIntosh commanded Company C at Fort Hays, since Captain John Tourtellotte was on detached service in Washington, D.C., as aide-de-camp to General Sherman.

McIntosh appeared before the board on November 11, 1870. His friend Lieutenant-Colonel Custer testified on his behalf. Custer told the board that McIntosh was a capable officer whose only offense was in antagonizing Colonel Sturgis. That testimony apparently swung the board, because McIntosh was not dismissed and rejoined Company G at Fort Lyon, Colorado Territory on February 11, 1871.

In 1871, another Canadian from what is now the province of Ontario joined the Seventh Cavalry: George Anderson of St. Catharines. St. Catharines is located near the United States border, near Niagara Falls. By the time Anderson was born, on June 14, 1842, construction of the Welland Canal was underway. The town, with a population of more than four thousand, had a Vigilance Society for the detection and punishment of horse thieves, and spa baths were created at the mineral springs.

Thousands of young Canadian men from border towns joined the army of the north in the U.S. Civil War, and their stories of adventure enticed many more south when the war was over. The town's proximity to the United States border, and the fact many people living in the area were from south of the border, may have contributed to Anderson's enlistment in the U.S. Army.

Twenty-nine-year-old Anderson was not a particularly imposing figure; light complexion, with light-coloured hair, he stood just over five-feet-five. The line of Anderson's history is not quite clear, but by 1871 he had already been in the army for five years, first signing up on September 16, 1866, just after the war between the states had ended.

With the army's new role in the Indian Wars, protecting immigration moving west, it's not surprising that Anderson joined the Seventh Cavalry for the adventure. Lieutenant John Weston enlisted him in Louisville, Kentucky, on August 16, 1871, enrolling him in Company K. But at the time of his enlistment, his company was sent to Yorkville, South Carolina, for its role in post-war reconstruction.

Edmond Tessier of Montreal, Quebec, was the next Canadian to sign up. He was a dark-skinned, dark-haired French Canadian, just topping five-foot-seven. In civilian life he had worked as a clerk, but he later chose to be a soldier. At the age of twenty-four, in 1871, he enlisted as a private in Yorkville, South Carolina, in the Seventh Cavalry, Company L. Company L was then sent to Fort Wallace, Kansas. Tessier's enlistment brought the number of Canadians in the Seventh to five.

That year, the Seventh Cavalry had been divided into small groups and distributed to posts in the south on reconstruction duty where there was civil unrest. The military wanted to seek out illegal distilleries and stamp out the Ku Klux Klan. Cooke was initially posted to Taylor Barracks, Louisville, Kentucky, as regimental adjutant. Lieutenant Donald McIntosh commanded Company G at Fort Lyon.

McIntosh was on the move over the next couple of years. In 1871 he was in a number of locations in South Carolina, finally in Spartenburg. Ku Klux Klan activity was heavy there, so Company G remained for nine months.

In 1872, he spent five months in Laurensville, Kentucky. McIntosh carried a diary or notebook, as many of the officers did. In it he kept a record of some of the minutiae of running a cavalry company, and the detail reflected his long years as a clerk for General Rucker in the quartermaster's department. The notes include a few days' payment to the Palmetto Hotel in Spartenburg of eighteen dollars, and twenty-five cents for a mule collar.

The diary shows a number of references to Sergeant John Vickory during that summer. The officer loaned Vickory ten dollars at Laurensville. Vickory was noted as being in charge of the "Manure Fund" during July and August. He was also in charge of buying fresh vegetables for the company.[4]

John Vickory was another Canadian who had served in the American Civil War before joining the Seventh Cavalry. William and Mariah Vickory Groesbeck lived in Toronto, Upper Canada, where John was born in 1847. The family moved to Clifton Park, New York, sometime shortly afterward, where his mother died in 1851.

Vickory had joined the army of the north as a teenager and had an irregular Civil War history. He was just sixteen years old when he enlisted under his own name, John H. Groesbeck, in Company H of the Fourteenth New York Heavy Artillery division on November 23, 1863.[5]

Groesbeck deserted from the Heavy Artillery the following spring, on April 23. He re-enlisted in Company H of the Second Massachusetts Cavalry a year later on May 10, 1864, but changed his name to John Vickory, probably to hide the fact he had deserted. There were no wide-spread identification checks in Civil War enlistments. He served until July 2, 1865. Vickory signed up in the regular army in Boston in 1866, at the age of nineteen, and again on September 9, 1869, pledging another five years.

In the Seventh Cavalry, Sergeant Vickory showed well in his cavalry blues. He had a dark complexion with blue eyes and brown hair. He was two inches short of six feet and in later years sported a bushy, dark moustache that all but hid his lips.

* * *

By January the next year McIntosh and his company were at Newberry, South Carolina. In an issue dated March 7, 1873, the *Columbia Daily Union* (South Carolina) wrote, "Company G arrived under the command of Lieutenants Wallace and McIntosh in town yesterday and the members paid off…. The list of arrivals at the Wheeler House [Columbia's newest hotel] included 'D. McIntosh 7ᵗʰ Cavalry.'"⁶

Company G spent time in Memphis, Tennessee, on the way north to Yankton, Dakota Territory. On May 7, 1873, Company G and nine other companies left Yankton for Fort Rice, first by rail then by horseback, up the Missouri River, 300 miles. They arrived just in time for the next mission.

Ten days later the Seventh Cavalry headed west on the Yellowstone Expedition. Throughout July they camped on the Yellowstone River near the mouth of the Powder River, all reinforcing Mollie's father's prediction of an unsettled soldier's life.

The troops had no large furniture or personal effects, and strikers, as soldier housemen were called, could pack up officers' quarters and have them on the move in less than two hours.

Mollie seemed to adapt well to the erratic, ever-changing army life, although it was far from what she had been used to. Her sister Katherine wrote, "It intrigued us quite a bit, back in Washington, D.C., to learn that my brother-in-law's troop had changed stations nine times in eleven months, and my mother's stationary soul suffered acutely at the thought of Mollie's perpetual home making and breaking."⁷

CHAPTER 11

THE NORTHERN PACIFIC RAILWAY

IT WAS THE DREAM OF A PHILADELPHIA FINANCIER THAT EVENtually took Custer, the Canadians, and the Seventh Cavalry to the northwest in 1973. His dream was to build a second transcontinental railway stretching from Lake Superior to Puget Sound on the Pacific. One of the major financiers of the north in the Civil War, Jay Cooke, had his eye on this line, and by the 1870s the work was underway, moving toward the Missouri River and a spot that is now Bismarck, North Dakota.

This move in the new republic of the United States prompted England and Canada to build the Canadian Pacific Railway to prevent the Americans from taking over the British Northwest. It also restarted the Sioux Indian fight against the white invasion of their territory. They realized the railway would destroy their way of life. Nomadic tribes had been compressed into the region, and they realized their hunting grounds were becoming smaller.

The Northern Pacific was running into the land of the Great Sioux warrior chief, Sitting Bull, who had about 1,000 warriors at any one time. He was already feeling pressure from the Crow tribe to the south and the Métis in the north. Although he had been defeated a number of times by white people, he was still an enemy to be reckoned with.

Jay Cooke considered himself a very religious man who believed he was "God's chosen instrument" and he would open up a railway between the mid-west and the Pacific Ocean.

By August 1871, two years before the Seventh Cavalry became a part of it, the Northern Pacific expedition survey had not yet reached the Yellowstone River valley. This left a gap of 600 miles between western Dakota Territory and eastern Montana. The company officials were afraid that Sitting Bull would come out against the surveyors. In June, company president J. Gregory Smith wrote to his leading civil engineer, W. Milnor Roberts, "It will probably be unsafe to carry on the work between the Missouri River and Bozeman Pass without a proper military escort. Negotiations are now underway to supply this, and it was hoped that sufficient military force will be detailed and placed at your disposal."[1]

Later that summer the military dispatched soldiers who were assigned to protect the workers. This permitted the Northern Pacific to enter the Yellowstone valley from the east where Fort Rice was built, and from the west at Fort Ellis. By early September, soldiers and surveyors were using Fort Rice as a jumping off post, twenty miles south of present-day Bismarck. West of this location the mapping was poor.

Jay Cooke chose Thomas Lafayette Rosser as chief engineer to lead his surveyors on this somewhat dangerous assignment. An ex-cavalryman, former Confederate general, thirty-five-year-old Rosser was an ideal candidate for the job. At over six feet, with dark wavy hair and bushy beard, he was an imposing figure. His storied career in the Civil War showed him to be a formidable leader.

Although born in Virginia his family had settled in Texas, and by the time war erupted he was a supporter of Texas secession. He was studying at West Point, along with Custer, before the war broke out, and, like Custer, left school just before graduation. But whereas Custer joined the northern army, Rosser joined the southern cause. He soon rose to the rank of colonel in the Fifth Virginia Cavalry.

Rosser fought in at least fifteen famous battles, showing he was not the kind to give up easily. At Antietam, his men screened General Robert E. Lee's forces, his actions were recognized at the second Battle of Bull Run, and he fought at Gettysburg.

At Trevilian Station, Rosser was part of a large group of cavalry officers who captured a number of prisoners from West Point classmate and close friend, George A. Custer. "Custer's total casualties were 416, including 41 dead and 242 captured"[2] (leaving 133 wounded or missing). That must have given Rosser some satisfaction. Custer's cook, Eliza, was also taken, but managed to escape from the wagon a couple of miles down the road. Later, on June 21, 1864, Custer wrote home to Libbie:

> Would you like to know what they have captured from me? *Everything except my toothbrush.* They only captured one wagon from me, (personally) but that contained my all — bedding, desk, sword-belt, underclothing, and my commission as General which only arrived a few days before; also dress coat, pants and one blue shirt.[3]

Rosser's brigade fought against Philip Sheridan in the Shenandoah Valley; the southern press tagged him with the nickname "Saviour of the Valley." He was promoted to major-general in November of 1864. In January he took 300 men across the mountains in deep snow to capture two northern infantry regiments at Beverly, West Virginia, taking 580 prisoners.

As General Robert E. Lee surrendered to the Union Army on April 9, 1865, Rosser escaped from Appomattox Camp with his command, finally surrendering himself at Staunton, Virginia, nearly a month later. Throughout the war Rosser was wounded three times, getting back into the saddle as soon as possible. He came out of the Civil War as major-general.

Rosser led the Northern Pacific Railway survey expedition when it left St. Paul, Minnesota, on August 28, 1871, and by September

7 it was at the Missouri River, opposite Fort Rice, without guides. At Fort Rice he met up with the Twenty-Second Infantry, the army contingent designated to guard the expedition.

The army escort was not as lucky as the survey team in its leader. He was Joseph Nelson Garland Whistler, first cousin of Whistler the artist, a heavy drinker who took his drinking and poker playing more seriously than his military duties.

The expedition party came to about 550 men, 375 of which were army members. Supplies were carried in 114 wagons for the sixty-day trip. As the Fort Rice band struck up "The Girl I Left Behind Me," the expedition set out on September 9.

The Dakota terrain was rugged, the rivers winding and the valleys covered with trees: cottonwood, maple, ash, and elm. Whistler and Rosser were often at odds on what route to take, with Whistler often leading them the wrong way. By late in the month they were getting into open fields with more signs of lignite coal and they could see large grass fires in the west, barely escaping one of them. Newspapers were reporting the disappearance of the Sioux from army posts and reservations, assuming they were getting ready to head off the survey party. There were more reports of the Indians setting the grass fires as a method of sidelining the railway expedition.

The survey party reached the badlands, the prairie giving way to the multi-coloured formations, the ridges dropping away, giving them spectacular views. What they needed was an exit on the western side of the Little Missouri River suitable for the railway tracks. It was like a maze through the badlands, but Rosser got lucky — a gap in the hills looked like an ideal route.

Around that time Rosser became sick. Whistler sent out a party of 235 men and supplies to search for a route to the Yellowstone River; he stayed in camp himself. But Rosser, although sick, led the party and found what he was looking for, twenty-eight miles from camp. Just past the place where the Bighorn River enters the Yellowstone, where the valley loses its rough landscape of buttes and becomes a landscape of cottonwoods and shrubbery, is the place at which he reached the Yellowstone River on October 3.

The party returned to Fort Rice, and on October 17 Rosser told his surveyors the expedition was over. The Northern Pacific had reached its goal without a confrontation with the Indian tribes.

By 1872 the company realized that last year's goal wasn't good enough; the railway needed a less expensive shortcut to the Yellowstone River. A tunnel was considered too expensive. Rosser led the survey party west again, this time protected only by the infantry. Colonel David Stanley led the escort of 586 officers and men with a twelve-pound Napoleon gun and three Gatling guns. His soldiers in woollen uniforms were faced with cloudless skies and 100-degree temperatures.

They were soon to meet up with a famed Indian leader known as Gall, sometimes written Gaul. He was tall, heavy-boned, and had a reputation as a skilled warrior and outstanding orator. Gall also had a reputation among the Indian tribes for his personal valour. He had been raised by Sitting Bull's father and had once beaten the Cheyenne warrior Roman Nose in a wrestling match.

Gall and his warriors attempted to block the 1872 survey. Rosser wrote of Gall's meeting with Stanley: Gall in full war regalia, wearing paint, breach cloth, and a stove pipe silk hat. "... This August prince of the plains was at once recognized as The Gaul, a minor chief of the Hunkpapa band of Sioux, distinguished for his cunning, cruelty, and courage. After the usual complaint, that we had invaded his country … he majestically ordered us to be gone."[4]

Farther to the west, another survey party led by John A. Haydon and a military escort led by Major Eugene Baker from Fort Ellis, was heading toward Yellowstone to meet up with the Rosser-Stanley expedition. Major Baker was another military man with a drinking problem.

Keeping a watch on all this was the great Sioux chief Sitting Bull. By mid-July of 1872 there were reported to be 2,000 Indian lodges on the Powder River near the Montana-Wyoming border, midway between the two survey parties. And on the night of August 13, in the midst of a war council, young warriors took their own lead. At three in the morning, 300 of them crossed the Yellowstone and opened fire on the Haydon-Baker campsite. Baker was in his tent "stupefied with drink." A young captain took over command and the Battle of Pryor Creek was on. There was a heavy exchange of shots in the dark but without much effect. Some well-armed prospectors and "wolfers" nearby joined the fray. Sitting Bull arrived and took up watch on a nearby bluff.

In an attempt to boost morale, Sitting Bull and two others walked slowly down the bluff at daylight and sat a few hundred yards away from the soldiers. Sitting Bull passed his pipe around. With bullets zipping by them, he slowly cleaned the pipe and walked back to the top of the bluff. In the end the Indians fled. Sitting Bull was defeated.

Haydon blamed Major Baker's lack of command throughout the expedition for his decision to abandon his western end of the survey. So in the long run Sitting Bull won that round, preventing Haydon and Rosser from joining up. The Indians still owned the Yellowstone River valley.

Meanwhile, on the eastern edge Rosser began his job of finding a more cost-effective shortcut through the low-lying badlands of eastern Montana. Stanley's drinking increased. He was apparently frustrated that he hadn't met up with Baker. He could wait, or go back and find out that Baker had made it through. They knew that Sitting Bull had joined up with Gall, which was also a worry for Stanley. He had no cavalry and could mount only about a dozen soldiers. On August 20, he decided to turn back toward Fort Rice.

Although Rosser probably didn't know yet, it was at this time that his young son Pelham died.

On the way back, Stanley was faced with a big problem at O'Fallon Creek Valley. It was ten miles long and didn't widen until Mildred, in what is now Montana. Once they entered the narrow confines of the valley there was no way out except the other end, ten miles away.

Sitting Bull knew that as well. The attack came at the narrowest point from about 200 Indians from nine different tribes. Stanley ordered the wagons into a circle, and the surveyors were told to keep inside. But at one point, the former confederate cavalry man, Rosser, jumped off his horse and stood by the Gatling gun "using [his] rifle vigorously." The Indians dispersed.

Both Rosser and Stanley were feeling low as the possibility of finding a shortcut to the Yellowstone River faded. Toward the end of September Rosser learned of his son's death. The soldiers were drinking excessively, most of them ragged and almost shoeless.

Some of the soldiers were sent ahead to Fort Rice, and the party remaining ran into some unexpected trouble. On October 3, Lieutenant Eban Crosby, who had lost his arm in the Civil War, went hunting on foot and was soon surrounded by Gall and a party of Hunkapapas. His death was slow and painful.

The next day Rosser himself had a close call. Venturing ahead to check out the survey line he found himself facing eighty hostile Indians. Aboard a wagon horse Rosser didn't have much of a chance to outrun them, but when others came to his rescue he hopped off his horse and sent what others called "a beautiful shot." It was a narrow escape for him. Lieutenant Louis Dent Adair of Stanley's Twenty-Second Regiment and Stephen Harris, Stanley's black servant, were both killed. Adair was the cousin of Julia Dent Grant, President Grant's wife.

News reports from these skirmishes, and especially of Adair's death, emphasized the risks associated with the Northern Pacific venture. The expedition was regarded as a public relations, and survey, failure.

Once again the survey team was laid off. Rosser returned to Minnesota.

* * *

The Northern Pacific Railway Company faced dire financial problems, both from lack of investors and company president Smith's excessive spending. By the end of the year the railway morale hit rock bottom with infighting, weakening bond sales, and rumours of Indian fighting. But Jay Cooke convinced people that the Northern Pacific could turn around; Smith had resigned, and Cooke said the company would forget the Yellowstone link, stop at the Missouri River, and avoid any more Indian fighting.

This all led to the idea of better army protection for the surveyors the next year, in 1873. It also would accomplish a goal for Sheridan and President Grant — it would give them a chance to punish the Sioux.

CHAPTER 12

THE SEVENTH CAVALRY HEADS NORTHWEST

JAY COOKE HAD PRESIDENT ULYSSES GRANT'S EAR, AND BY THE summer of 1873, when the Seventh Cavalry entered the picture, the surveying was underway again between Bismarck and Yellowstone River in Montana.

This was the year that Northern Pacific wanted to accomplish two goals: complete the track to the present day Bismarck in what was then Dakota Territory and finally finish the Yellowstone mapping in a line of survey from Lake Superior to Puget Sound; and find a shortcut west of Bismarck, avoiding extensive construction along the eastern half of the Heart River.

General Sheridan had a plan of his own. He wanted to build one or two military posts along the railway line between the crossing of the Missouri River and the mouth of the Powder. He outlined his plan to Rosser at a meeting in Chicago. Sheridan would assemble 2,000 men at Fort Rice and Buford. On reaching the Yellowstone River at Glendive, the soldiers would march up river to Pompey's Pillar, cross to Musselshell, loop east to Yellowstone, and return, selecting fort sites on the way.

On February 23, Rosser wrote to Roberts that, "Sheridan is very earnest and his preparations to protect our surveying parties during the summer are very elaborate." Rosser must have appreciated the change from his dealings with the previous military leaders who tended to drink away any challenges or problems.

Sheridan would get $250,000 in federal funding for the forts, if and when the Northern Pacific pushed forward. He also succeeded in getting the Seventh Cavalry transferred to the department of Dakota.

* * *

The next Canadian to join the Seventh had an important job. He was saddler George Hayward. The cavalry men spent most of their working lives on their horses in their saddles. They depended on saddles for fit, comfort, and workability. In the 1850s George McClellan designed the McClellan saddle for the United States cavalry. The saddle was developed so that the tree or base was fitted to the rider's seat as well as the horse's back. Leather straps, connecting the stirrups to the saddle tree, protected the rider's legs from horse sweat. Another important strap went round the horse's barrel or belly to hold the saddle on.

It was May 13, 1873, when twenty-two-year-old Hayward enlisted. Hayward was from Walton, Ontario, just east of the shores of Lake Huron. He had worked as a harness maker before joining, and signed up as a saddler in Company I in St. Louis. His job was to keep the troopers happy in their saddles and to make sure their equipment was always in good working order.

In 1873 the Seventh Cavalry gained a new life. It was reunited in Dakota Territory outside the states. After two years of relatively quiet times in Elizabethtown, Custer headed once again into the field; into Indian country. The new role of the Seventh was to guard the engineers of the Northern Pacific Railway while they surveyed the westward route to the Yellowstone River.

Earlier that spring on April 9, 1873, when the Seventh was first ordered to Dakota Territory, it rode into Yankton, the territorial capital, on the Dakota Southern Railroad from Sioux City, Iowa. Custer had with him 800 troops, 700 horses, 202 mules, enlisted men's and officers' families, and aides. During the encampment in Yankton, a ball was given in honor of Custer and his officers, with music provided by a local band.

The leader of the band that night was a lithe, trim, thirty-nine-year-old Italian named Felix Vinatieri, who led the band with gusto. General Custer thought the music sophisticated for a wilderness town and asked to meet the band leader. He [Custer] explained that his present leader had requested to be relieved. The General liked Felix Vinatieri, and offered him the position of Chief Musician.[1]

By the age of ten, Felix Vinatieri, born in Turin, Italy, was already an accomplished violinist. He graduated from a Naples conservatory of music, and by twenty he was director of an Italian military band. Five years later, he immigrated to America and enlisted with the Sixteenth Regiment of Massachusetts at Boston. He served in the Civil War, was sent west, and discharged in December 1870 in Dakota Territory. Vinatieri settled in Yankton. He married Anna Fejfar, from a music-loving Czechoslovakian immigrant family, and set up a studio to teach and compose music.

The Seventh's military band rode out of Yankton for Fort Abraham Lincoln on May 7, 1973. Felix Vinatieri sat on the lead horse. After arriving at the fort, thirty-nine-year-old Vinatieri travelled to St. Paul, Minnesota, to enlist for a three-year period as bandleader for the Seventh Cavalry.

At the tiny post of Fort Rice, on the Missouri River in Dakota Territory, there was no accommodation for the army wives. All of them, including Elizabeth Custer, had to travel back the way they came. Lizzie Custer was going home to Monroe, Michigan.

The Seventh Cavalry was now in the field as military escort to the survey expedition for the proposed Northern Pacific Railway line, accompanied by its regimental band.

A surprise awaited Custer — an old friend from his West Point days and an enemy on the Confederate side during the Civil War. Ex-cavalryman Thomas Rosser once again headed up the survey team. Custer recounted the meeting in a letter to his wife on June 26, 1873, from a camp on Heart River, Dakota Territory, just six days after leaving Fort Rice.

Well, I have joined the engineers. The day we arrived I was lying half asleep when I heard "Orderly, which is General Custer's tent?" I sprang up. "I know that voice even if I haven't heard it for years!" It was my old friend Genl. Rosser. Stretched on a buffalo robe under a fly in the moonlight, we listened to one another's accounts of the battles in which we had been opposed. It seemed like the time when, as cadets, we lay, huddled under one blanket, indulging in dreams of the future.

Rosser said the worst whipping he ever had was that of Oct. 9th (Well I do remember it) when I captured everything he had, including that uniform of his now in Monroe. He said he had been on a hill, watching our advance, and, through his field-glasses, recognized me, so sent for his Brigade-Commander, and said, "Do you see that long-haired man in the lead? Well, that's Custer, and we are going to bust him up" ... and so we should have only you slipped another column round us, and soon my men were crying out "We're flanked, We're flanked."[2]

There was no mention in the letter of Rosser capturing hundreds of Custer's men in the Civil War Trevilian Raid.

On the expedition Rosser was still having trouble with General Stanley in command of the infantry, Stanley having been found "dead drunk on the ground outside the camp."

> Rosser said he told General S. in St. Paul before starting that he [Stanley] would have a different man to deal with this year, in command of the 7th Cav. — one who would not hesitate, as second in command, to put a guard over him, S., if incapacitated....[3]

By July the expedition had reached the Yellowstone River in Montana Territory. The Yellowstone flows from the Missouri River in a northeast direction. This was a land of petrified trees, high out-croppings of rock, and fossil finds. The cavalry marched westward in search of a supply steamer that was to meet the expedition at Glendive Creek. Often having to re-trek around bluffs blocking their way, they finally came to the mouth of Glendive Creek where the steamer *Key West* was tied up at a depot of supplies, and with 180 infantry on board.[4]

McIntosh and Company G were part of the expedition. At the end of June, he noted in his diary that there was $112.33 in the post company fund. In July, he paid just four dollars for a couple of horses for himself, and kept a running account of minor stores for his company.

The other Canadians — Edmund Tessier, George Anderson, and George Hayward — were also with the expedition, travelling through the wide open spaces and buttes of Montana, a far cry from the treed landscape of Upper and Lower Canada. Tessier had spent the last few years with Company L at Fort Wallace, Kansas, under the command of First Lieutenant Henry J. Nowlan. Anderson was with Company K under the command of Captain Owen Hale at Yorkville, South Carolina, and Hayward with Company I commanded by Captain Myles W. Keogh stationed at Bagdad, Kentucky.

By early August the regiment had made some Indian sightings. Custer was out on patrol with about eighty cavalrymen when he became aware of a party of Indians ahead. These were soon dispersed but the Natives watched the column of soldiers from the bluffs for nearly a week. On August 4, the column approached the mouth of the Rosebud River, about three miles below the mouth of the Little Bighorn River. This was about twenty miles from Sitting Bull's camp, which held between 300 and 400 lodges.

The Hunkpapas were under Gall, and the Oglalas were under Crazy Horse. Some of the Natives were Cheyennes from Black Kettle's old band who had survived the Battle of Washita. They decided to trap Custer and the Seventh. But by this time Custer was aware of Indian tactics and the danger of being lured into a trap. Seeing Custer, and apparently with Black Kettle in mind, the Cheyennes charged out of the bush too early, ending the chance of an ambush.

The fighting lasted three hours in 100 degree heat, ending with the Indians fleeing.

On August 8, Stanley agreed with Custer to follow the fleeing Sitting Bull villages that had now crossed the Yellowstone. More Indians were joining Sitting Bull on the other side. The battle in the early morning hours of August 11 had the Natives crossing the river and trying to catch Custer's men in crossfire. One unit of twenty men was soon facing 100 Indians, including Gall and possibly Crazy Horse. Three companies of reinforcements, E, K, and L, which included Anderson and Tessier, arrived, and the Indians fell back.

Just after eight that same morning, Custer decided to launch a counterattack, ordering Lieutenant McIntosh and Company G to hold the ground between the river and the camp. Stanley then appeared with reinforcements. True to his style, Custer then ordered the Seventh Cavalry band forward. It struck up the "Garry Owen," and Custer, leading almost 300 men, ordered the charge. At this, the Indians turned and fled.

Custer later wrote of the role played by Donald McIntosh and his Company in dispersing the 300 Indians.

Lieutenant McIntosh, commanding "G" Company, moved his command up the valley at a gallop, and prevented many of the Indians from crossing. The chase was continued with utmost vigor until the Indians were completely dispersed and driven a distance of nine miles from where the engagement took place, and they were here forced back across the Yellowstone....[5]

General Stanley describes the action in his report to the War Department August, 1873.

On the 10th they discovered that the Indians had crossed the Yellowstone in skin boats, rafts, three miles below the mouth of the Little Big Horn.

Custer tried industriously to cross, but the river is deep and swift, and American horses do not take it.

Next morning the Indians fired across the river [about 700 ft. wide] and Custer found himself assailed from a bluff, 600 yards to the rear. Pushing up a skirmish line in that direction, he formed each squadron into a separate column, and charged, driving them [the Indians] 6 to 10 miles from the field.[6]

Custer then separated from the main party, taking six companies of the Seventh Cavalry and advancing about 150 miles through unknown territory with the railway engineers. He left Companies F and L behind to accompany Stanley, which meant Tessier was left behind. The two parties were united at the Yellowstone, and the Seventh had crossed to the east side on the steam boat *Josephine* by September 10.

The Seventh headed east, leaving Stanley and the rest of the expedition party on the other side of the Yellowstone. Early in the summer they had left from Fort Rice, and on September 21 arrived at the new Fort Abraham Lincoln on the west shore of the Missouri River, across from Bismarck, the territorial capital of Dakota. The Bismarck Tribune noted Custer's arrival at the new fort in his wartime outfit that had "so often startled the corn-fed Johnnies ... the well remembered plain blue pants, with their yellow stripe, the blue flannel shirt, with its wide collar and cuffs, loose at the throat, the black slouch and the jingling spurs."[7]

Rosser was able to bask in glory for a short period. His new survey cut a little over twenty-three miles from the proposed rail line, and it looked like construction would start the next year.

Custer took leave to bring his wife and sister from Monroe to the fort. Fort Abraham Lincoln was a military island surrounded by "hostile" Indians. It was remote, and it was bitter cold in winter. They arrived in November to the tune of the regimental band.

The Seventh Cavalry at Fort Abraham Lincoln, Dakota Territory, 1873. At the right, both standing, are Molly McIntosh and Lieutenant Donald McIntosh.

Courtesy of Denver Public Library, Western Collection, B425.

CHAPTER 13

THE MCINTOSH HOUSEHOLD

IT WAS IN THE SPRING OF 1874 THAT THE TRAIN PULLED INTO Bismark around five o'clock in the afternoon, ending a long journey of many days from Washington, D.C., for Katherine Garrett. Katherine, known as Katie, was the younger sister of Mollie Garrett McIntosh, who was also on board. Katie had been ill over the winter and hadn't managed to overcome the cough. After much discussion, her widowed mother agreed Katie should visit Mollie and Donald, taking advantage of the clear, dry air of the west to cure the problem. Mollie had travelled east in Dakota Territory to meet her sister and they both stepped down from the train at Bismarck. Katie wrote in her diary of that meeting, notes later used in a book by her daughter:

> Suddenly from behind a wooden pillar, stepped the tall, lithe figure of an army officer in uniform, wearing a forage cap which bore the number 7, and a pair of shoulder straps showing the insignia of a first lieutenant....
>
> He hurried toward us, and, as I looked into his strong, purposeful face and kindly, dark eyes, I suddenly knew that Mollie was a very lucky woman....
>
> Donald smiled and snow-white teeth flashed from behind his thin lips.[1]

A military ambulance delivered them to the fort. Fort Lincoln was set in a valley flanked by bluffs; an infantry post sat guard there.

The barracks were built on the side of the parade grounds nearest the river and the officers' quarters faced the other direction. A granary and a small military prison made up the left of the parade ground, with the quartermaster buildings and adjutant office completing the square. The horse stables were outside this square. The McIntosh quarters were on Officers' Row, a detached frame house accommodating two families. The wind blew through the cracks in the walls:

> It was lighted by kerosene lamps and candles, and the walls of the medium-sized living room were hung with old canvas tenting to make the place warmer. A lighted stove in the middle of the room threw out grateful heat. A few campstools and unpainted chairs were scattered around, and a fur rug or two served as floor coverings.
>
> The only piece of furniture that lifted this atmosphere of dreariness was a piano that Mollie had shipped from St. Paul.... On top of the instrument sprawled a Martin guitar, a banjo, and a violin. The dining room beyond displayed another stove and a table made of three wooden planks stretched across two carpenter's horses. This type of table served several purposes in those old army days, such as a bed, an ironing board, and a bench.[2]

Katie Garrett soon became part of the McIntosh family and the bigger family of the Custer officers. The McIntosh home, or tent in the field, drew the young officers and wives. Often they would gather there while Molly and Katie played their guitars and led a sing song. Katie described Donald as having a quiet voice and manner, with a keen sense of humour. She marked him as one of the most beloved officers of the regiment. "He combined the brilliant mind of a student with a marked flair for military science, and to his friends he was affectionately known as 'Tosh.' Personally I loved him as my own brother."[3]

Katie Garrett also enjoyed the spectacle of the formal parade and retreat, which the cavalry performed even in far-off Dakota Territory. There was a parade ground within the fort, but Custer, ever the showman, would put on a full-dress mounted affair on the level plain at the outskirts of the garrison. This spectacle brought an audience, not only from outlying infantry posts, but ranchmen from neighboring ranches, Indians from the reservation, and even people from across the river in Bismarck. They arrived in buckboards, wagons, or by horse.

The companies of the Seventh mounted on glossy well-groomed horses, with the men wearing black helmets with chin straps, decorated with gold spread-eagles and thick yellow plumes on gold spikes. Their uniforms were of blue and gold with sabres hung at the side. The officers' uniforms were trimmed with golden epaulets and gold thread sabre belts; heavy gold cords and tassels were worn across the breast. Yellow stripes ran down the trousers into high-topped boots.

Ranking officers and sergeants bawled out the orders, and the columns swept by with flags flying. They formed and divided in trots or gallops, to the tune of the commands or bugle calls, a display for Custer, but also a display of authority and strength for the onlookers; giving comfort to the far flung ranchers, and possibly striking fear in the Indians.

CHAPTER 14

THE INDIANS
AND THE BLACK HILLS

THE BLACK HILLS OF THE PRESENT DAY SOUTH DAKOTA ROLL into the border with Wyoming. They cover an area of about 6,000 square miles, the highest elevation being Harney Point at 7,242 feet. They are the tallest peaks in continental North America east of the Rockies. The name comes from the Lakota, or Teton Sioux, words *Paha Sapa*, meaning "hills that are black," because of the dark appearance from a distance.

By the time of the American Revolution in the late 1770s, the Sioux claimed land many times the size of the eastern seaboard colonies. Their land included part of what would become five states: Minnesota, Iowa, North Dakota, Nebraska, and most of South Dakota. Not that they kept to these boundaries; they roamed where the buffalo roamed, into Canada and as far south as Texas.

By pushing out other tribes, the Sioux moved as far west as the Black Hills, claiming them for their own. The shale gave the hills a silvery face. With their fresh mountain streams, trees for lodge poles, and medicine plants for healing, the Black Hills became a holy place for the Sioux. They venerated the Hills and threatened any member who revealed the existence of gold.

The California Gold Rush of 1849 and the Oregon Trail cutting through Sioux territory, moving immigration west, led to the signing of the first treaty of Laramie in 1851. This included government payment to the Indians, binding the Sioux to a dependent way of life and setting boundaries on their land. Clashes with the government and the military were inevitable as white men invaded the territory for gold and land. When it came to a choice between the Natives and supporting the immigrants moving west, inevitably treaty promises were broken.

Hostilities escalated during the Civil War, including the Chivington-led massacre of Indians at Sand Creek, Colorado. In 1866, the government negotiated a $70,000 annuity with the Sioux for the Bozeman Trail, which stretched from Fort Laramie, Wyoming, through Sioux land. These negotiations did not include all chiefs, and certainly not all the young warriors were in agreement. Many Natives had no wish to be dependent, to till the land, nor to be restricted in their movements.

Nor did most of the military agree with the deals. The Sioux could expect no soft approach by the military commander in the west, General Sherman, who had demonstrated his ruthlessness in the Civil War when his army plundered the Georgia countryside in his scorch-and-burn march to the sea. In Washington there was an ongoing battle over whether or not it was the military or Indian Affairs department that would have the final say regarding the Indians. General Sherman watched the buffalo herds dwindle and the railway move west as good signs for his side.

The Hills had not yet been explored to any extent, but were on the trails leading to the gold fields of the far west. And there were rumours of hidden wealth regarding the Hills themselves; the lure of gold had already drawn adventurous panhandlers and settlers to the area.

Indian tribes on the western plains often fought among themselves, but by 1866 they were beginning to unite in their opposition to inroads being made by the white people on their lands. Sioux chief Red Cloud gave them a rallying cry, calling the white man's encroachment "an insult to the spirits of our ancestors. Are we then to give up their sacred graves to be plowed for corn? Dakotas, I am for war!"[1]

There were many prominent chiefs and warriors on the plains. Sioux Chief Gall had long been recognized among his people as a brave leader and warrior. He had grown up with a reputation as a great athlete and was considered a good strategist. One of the stories spreading his fame was a wrestling match with an equally powerful Cheyenne boy, Roman Nose. It was the custom of the northwestern Indians, if they camped together, to establish the athletic supremacy of the youth. On a plateau between the two camps the young boys would line up facing each other and wrestle to the ground. On this occasion Gall and Roman Nose were the last two standing.

> Finally by trick or main force, Gall laid the other sprawling upon the ground and held him fast for a minute, then released him and stood erect,... Shout after shout went up on the Sioux side of the camp. The mother of Roman Nose came forward and threw a superbly worked buffalo robe over Gall, whose mother returned the compliment by covering the young Cheyenne [Roman Nose]with a handsome blanket.
> ... It was his [Gall's] habit to appear most opportunely in a crisis, and in a striking and dramatic manner take command of the situation....[2]

Gall upheld the Indian rights to the buffalo plains and wanted the government to stay strictly to its agreements.

It was the disregard of the 1868 treaty that prompted Chief Gall, one of the most aggressive leaders of the Sioux nation, to support Sitting Bull in defending the Indians once vast domain.[3]

It was just at the age of sixteen that Crazy Horse made his name through saving the life of an older warrior and friend, Hump, in a battle against another tribe. Hump's horse was shot from under him. In a shower of arrows Crazy Horse leaped from his own pony, helped his friend into the saddle, jumped up behind him, and road him off to safety. This was just the first of a number of stories telling of his bravery in battle. The young warrior was known for his hunting prowess as well.

Crazy Horse had had his "great vision quest" in the Black Hills as a boy and they were sacred ground to him. "One does not sell the land on which the people walk," said Crazy Horse, who, unlike the loquacious Sitting Bull, spoke briefly when he spoke at all.[4]

But it was Sitting Bull, a member of the Hunkpapa band of Sioux, whose fame spread in the American west. The many stories about the chief began early on with his naming. After a buffalo hunt the Indian boys would often have a mimic hunt with the calves left behind. At one of these Sitting Bull was thrown from his horse and a large calf turned on him. The boy struggled with the calf, pushing it back by the ears until it sat down. From then on he was given the name Sitting Bull.

He depended on the warrior Crazy Horse to win his battles, while he directed his energies to tribal affairs. It was Sitting Bull's strong personality that helped hold the many hostile Indian tribes together as a unit against the whites.

By 1863 Sitting Bull was convinced it was time to oppose the white man's spread into Indian Territory. The Minnesota Sioux had risen up against the whites and murdered many settlers, then fled into the Hunkpapa's area appealing for help. Sitting Bull was convinced of their cause, joined forces with the renegade Minnesota Sioux, and was acknowledged as a leader.

In 1865 and 1866 he met the Canadian half-breed, Louis Riel, instigator of two rebellions, who had come across the [border] line for safety; and in fact at this time he [Sitting Bull] harbored a number of outlaws and fugitives from justice. His conversations with these, especially with the French mixed-bloods, who inflamed his prejudices against the Americans, also had their influence in making of the wily Sioux a determined enemy to the white man.[5]

Courtesy of Denver Public Library, Western collection, x31691.

Sioux Hunkpapa Chief Sitting Bull,
spiritual leader of the Plains Indians.
Sitting Bull had been a great warrior.

In what is called the Red Cloud Wars, the Indians decided to keep control of the Powder River country of Wyoming. The Teton Sioux chiefs, of the western or plains dwellers known as the horse Indians, met and advocated strong resistance to the encroachment of white men and their forts into Indian Territory. They decided to defend their rights by force. Sitting Bull used his strong personality to hold the Indians together. He depended on twenty-one-year-old Crazy Horse to lead his forces in the field. At the Indian council on the Powder River, Sitting Bull is quoted as saying:

> We have now to deal with another people, small and feeble when our forefathers first met with them but now great and overbearing.... the love of possessions is a disease in them....
>
> My brothers, shall we submit? Or shall we say to them: 'First kill me, before you can take possession of my fatherland!'[6]

In the 1860s a number of forts had been built in the area to protect the miners travelling north on the Oregon Trail to present-day Montana. Colonel Henry Beebe Carrington was sent west to establish the forts, Reno, Phil Kearny, and C.F. Smith.

Fort Phil Kearny sat on the east side of Big Horn Mountains along the Bozeman Trail in what is now northeast Wyoming. The largest of three forts in the area, it was nestled in the foothills of the Big Horn mountains and along Piney Creek. An eight-foot high palisade of sharpened logs protected it. A few miles away, up the slopes of the Big Horns, two lumber camps were set up to provide construction and firewood for the fort.

Red Cloud launched his attacks with the combined warriors of the Lakota, Cheyenne, and Arapaho. Woodcutters, military patrols, small parties of emigrants, and gold miners were killed in these forays.

Captain William J. Fetterman arrived at the fort in November of 1866.

> Fetterman, a much-decorated hero of the Civil War who had held the brevet rank of lieutenant-colonel of volunteers, was angered and frustrated by the situation he found there. How dare the Indians hold the U.S. government at bay?... Much of Fetterman's ire was directed at his commander, whom he deemed timid and overly cautious.... Fetterman loudly derided the enemy as simple savages and boasted, "With 80 men I could ride through the Sioux nation!"[7]

By December 21, the last load of firewood was scheduled to be moved from the Big Horn forest to Fort Phil Kearny. The wagons were attacked by the Sioux and Cheyenne warriors. Carrington dispatched a relief party of infantry reinforced by Company C of the

Second Cavalry. Captain Fetterman insisted on taking command. Carrington warned him not to be lured over Lodge Trail Ridge, out of distance from the main command

As Fetterman rushed to assist the wagon train carrying the wood, Red Cloud's attackers fled in front of the relief party, drawing them farther and farther from the fort — all in accordance with Red Cloud's plan. As the relief party hesitated on Lodge Trail Ridge, a daring warrior turned back to taunt the soldiers. That did the trick. Fetterman's soldiers plunged down the far side in pursuit. Within minutes the snowy slopes were alive with hundreds of Indian warriors. It was a short and brutal fight. Within the hour, before soldiers from the fort could ride to the rescue, Captain Fetterman lay dead with his entire command, all eighty men, many cut up beyond recognition.

The young warrior who lured Fetterman's command over Lodge Trail Ridge was Crazy Horse.

The government called it the Fetterman Massacre; to the Indians it was the Battle of the Hundred Slain. It was a replica of the Sand Creek Massacre, but this time it was the whites who died. And Red Cloud kept up his advantage.

As the siege dragged on, the soldiers at Fort Phil Kearny became increasingly isolated and desperate. Red Cloud continued his war; maintaining the fragile alliance of tribes while at the same time keeping the Army besieged ... In August the following year, he launched what he hoped would be a devastating assault on a small woodcutting party. What he couldn't have anticipated was that these 31 men were armed with the new breech-loading rifles. The Indian attackers died by the score. But Red Cloud had made his point and the United States government decided to negotiate for peace.[8]

Washington set up a peace commission to negotiate the treaty. In late 1867, it met with nine bands of Sioux at North Platte, Nebraska. General Sherman made his point known in the peace talks. Chief Spotted Tail said the Indians objected to the Powder River Road, which was driving away their game, and called on the government to leave the road. General Sherman answered on the Commission's behalf.

> The United States cannot abandon its road across your country but it will pay any damage done by the Bozeman Trail....
>
> The railroads are coming and you cannot stop [them] any more than you can stop the sun or the moon. You must decide; you must submit. This is not a peace commission only; it's a war commission.[9]

Red Cloud's answer was to continue the Bozeman Trail raids along with a number of others, including Crazy Horse and Gall. And by spring of 1868 Washington had come up with a peace treaty containing almost everything Red Cloud had wanted — what became known as the Laramie Treaty.

Article 2 of the treaty gave the Indians all of present-day South Dakota west of the Missouri River, including the Black Hills. It was Article 16 that gave the Great Sioux Reservation the contested Powder River country "north of the Platte and east of the summits of the Big Horn Mountains," where no white man could set foot without Indian consent.

There was also an area where there were already white settlements; the treaty granted the Sioux hunting rights there "so long as the buffalo may range thereon in such numbers as to justify the chase."

> Article 16. The United States hereby agrees and stipulates that the country north of the North Platte River

and east of the summits of the Big Horn Mountains shall be held and considered to be unceded Indian territory, and also stipulates and agrees that no white person or persons shall be permitted to settle upon or occupy any portion of the same ... the military posts now established in the territory in this article named shall be abandoned, and that the road leading to them and by them to the settlements in the territory of Montana shall be closed.[10]

Sitting Bull had already signed. Red Cloud was the last to sign, insisting that all the forts in the territory be vacated before he would do so. Orders were issued to close the forts. Fort Kearny, the site of the Fetterman Massacre, wasn't abandoned until late summer. Red Cloud's warriors torched the empty forts.

Red Cloud came into Fort Laramie to sign the treaty in November of 1868. He made the price of peace clear: the road was to be closed and the Sioux free to roam and hunt. The Sioux had won this round.

The Treaty of Fort Laramie in Wyoming guaranteed the Black Hills to the Lakotas. It gave them hunting rights in South Dakota, Wyoming, and Montana. The wording indicated no one except those designated within the treaty would be permitted to pass over or settle in the territory. The land would be closed to whites unless allowed by the Sioux; it would ensure their civilization, and had financial incentives for them to farm the land.

But not everyone had the same perspective. The Indians thought they could roam and hunt freely, Washington thought it would lead to them peacefully farming the land, and General Sherman thought "peace within the reservation and war without."

Soon afterwards three chiefs, Sitting Bull, Red Cloud and Spotted Tail, visited Washington, dining with President Ulysses S. Grant. Sitting Bull hoped to preserve the Big Horn and Black Hills country for the Indians as permanent hunting grounds.

He considered that the life of the white man as he saw it was no life for his people, but hoped by close adherence to the terms of this treaty to preserve the Big Horn and Black Hills country for a permanent hunting ground. When gold was discovered and the irrepressible gold seekers made their historic dash across the plains into this forbidden paradise, then his faith in the white man's honor was gone forever.... [11]

In May 1870, Red Cloud and Spotted Tail travelled to Washington. Red Cloud gave a lengthy, passionate speech about his people — a story of broken treaties, swindles, liquor, roads and railways, poverty, and war:

Tell the Great Father [President Ulysses Grant] to move Fort Fetterman away and we will have no more troubles. I have two mountains in that country [the Black Hills and Big Horn Mountains]. I want the Great Father to make no roads through them....

I don't want my reservation on the Missouri ... Our children are dying off like sheep. The country does not suit them.... [12]

Red Cloud's peace brought new efforts by the Indian Department to bring about more agencies and make the Indians more dependent, but it received mixed reviews back home, particularly from Hunkpapa Chief Sitting Bull. He said the more docile Indians were fools to sell their livelihood for bacon, sugar, and coffee.

The government could see no progress in ensuring peace while much of the Sioux tribe lived off more than a million dollars worth of rations, and Washington made no effort to stop violations of the 1868 treaty. An indication of just how the government viewed the situation appears in a letter written by the very man who was responsible for Sioux territorial rights in the region. In a letter to the Department of the Dakotas on March 28, 1872, Secretary of the Interior Columbus Delano wrote:

> I am inclined to think that the occupation of this region of the country is not necessary to the happiness and prosperity of the Indians, and as it is supposed to be rich in minerals and lumber it is deemed important to have it freed as early as possible from Indian occupancy. I shall, therefore, not oppose any policy which looks first to a careful examination of the subject … If such an examination leads to the conclusion that country is not necessary or useful to Indians, I should then deem it advisable…to extinguish the claim of the Indians and open the territory to the occupation of the whites.[13]

Meanwhile, General Sheridan was gearing up to bring the issue to a final resolution. Both the government and the U.S. Army had plans for not only getting through the uncharted hills, but also exploring them for any minerals that might be worthwhile. And there seemed to be a general feeling that too much land had been allotted to too few Sioux; those numbers were estimated at 15,000 to 25,000 Indians in 1872.

CHAPTER 15

A NEW ASSIGNMENT

B Y 1874 THE NORTHERN PACIFIC RAILWAY'S PUSH TO THE northwest had come to a halt. Both the driving force behind the scheme, Jay Cooke, and the company itself, had declared bankruptcy. The company was in trouble with its investors, and Custer's written account of the summer expedition in the *New York Tribune*, September 6, 1873, seemed to exacerbate the financial panic.

> With unerring instinct Custer understated his role, credited subordinates, overstated Indian prowess, magnified dangers, and left the reader with the knowledge — without ever stating it — that victory had been achieved only through exceptional leadership: his.[1]

And a few days later the *New York Times* followed this up:

> If several thousand of our best soldiers, with all the arms of the service, under some of our most dashing officers, can only hold the ground on their narrow line of march for 150 or 200 miles west of the Upper Missouri, [what] will peaceful bodies of railroad workmen be able to do, or what can emigrants accomplish in such a dangerous region?[2]

On September 18, the panic began. Stocks and bonds began falling, and many banks shut their doors. On Wall Street in New York City, people poured out into the street.

In Minneapolis Tom Rosser wrote in his diary: "Learned that Jay Cooke & co. had failed and the future of our company is dark and uncertain." Rosser laid off contractors he had just hired, somehow got his men paid, and packed his reports and maps — which were not to be needed until the end of the decade.[3]

The newspaper answered its own question, saying the Sioux must be taught a lesson and forced to submit. The uncertainty was enough to frighten investors, and the Northern Pacific adventure was at a temporary standstill. This was to the liking of General Phil Sheridan, U.S. Army. He could now focus on his main interest: forcing the Plains Indians onto reservations and freeing the west for immigration.

The government in Washington, D.C., decided that military protection was needed for the many immigrants who were now making their way into the northwest. General Sheridan, commander of the Division of the Missouri, in consultation with General Alfred Terry, commander of the department of Dakota under him, advised setting up a series of army posts, a case of déjà vu. Sheridan turned to a former member of his staff and veteran Indian fighter. On June 10, 1874, he wrote from Chicago to Major Sandy Forsyth:

The reconnaissance to be made by Lt-Col George A. Custer to the Black Hills will leave Ft. Abraham Lincoln on or about the 25th June, and I wish you to proceed to that point and to report in person to Genl. Custer, to accompany it.

It is especially desirable that these Headquarters should have a complete and detailed description of the country passed over, so it is desired that you will devote yourself to the collection of such information, and embody it in a daily diary.

This should embrace distance travelled, character of the soil, wood, water and grass, and topography or surface and geological information, as well as incidents which may occur.

On the return of the command to Ft. Abraham Lincoln you will proceed without delay to report in person to these Headquarters.[4]

The expedition was organized in compliance with Department of Dakota, Special Orders No. 117:

Reconnoitering the route from that post [Fort Lincoln] to Bear Butte, in the Black Hills, and exploring the country south, southeast, and southwest of that point. The expedition will consist of six companies of the Seventh Cavalry, now stationed at Fort Abraham Lincoln; the four companies of the same regiment now at Fort Rice; Company I, Twentieth Infantry; and Company C, Seventeenth Infantry; ... [5]

The ten companies of the Seventh Cavalry, and two companies of infantry, with a detachment of Indian scouts, prepared for the push into the Black Hills of South Dakota. Fort Abraham Lincoln was a six-company post; the other detachments were at Fort Rice a few miles away. Fort Rice was a stockade in a desolate area on the banks of the Missouri river. Katie Garrett called it "one of the most Godforsaken spots on earth."

A training camp had been selected two miles south of Fort Abraham Lincoln for the reunion of the regimental companies. There, in an area of wood, grass, and level country with plenty of water nearby, there would be several weeks of training of new recruits before the command set out.

At Fort Abraham Lincoln, supply wagons were packed with sacks of potatoes, kitchen utensils, axes, and shovels, with some full of hay and fodder. Saddlers such as George Hayward of Walton, Upper Canada, sewed up everything, including bedding, into canvas rolls. Guns and ammunition were packed into other wagons. Cattle to be killed along the way on the expedition were herded in place. But Hayward didn't make the expedition — his Company I stayed back at the fort. In all, about 1,200 men and 110 wagons along with artillery and two months worth of food supply moved out for the expedition.

In the McIntosh house everyone prepared. Donald McIntosh's striker laid out his uniform, "troop boots uniform trousers, a blue flannel shirt, a wide-brimmed, black felt hat, cartridge belt, and revolver." The officers' wives accompanied the regiment to camp. They rode in ambulance wagons. Mollie and Katie were in one, with Mollie's cook, Iwilla, holding six hams she'd cooked the day before.

The move to camp was made in an impressive ceremony. With Custer mounted and at the head of the column and Vinatieri leading the band, the trumpeter blew the call for mounting, "Boots and Saddles," and the men took to their saddles. The band led the way as the troops rode in double file behind Custer and the officers. Camp equipment, supply wagons drawn by mules, cattle, and the quartermaster's group brought up the rear. They rolled out for camp on June 10, 1874.

Hordes of dogs surrounded the column, the General
and Tom owning forty of them. The cavalcade was so
long that it took us nearly two hours to reach camp,

but once there the wheels of military efficiency revolved like those of a well-oiled clock. Along the company streets tents were erected and furnished with cots, campstools, tin basins, buckets, dippers and small mirrors swinging crazily from center poles;...

The canvas of the commanding officer was set a little apart from the rest, but he enjoyed no more luxuries than his subalterns.[6]

As the new camp was being set up, a column of soldiers appeared around the bend in the road. At the sight of the Fort Rice detachment a roar of welcome went up and the band swung into "Garry Owen," the Seventh Cavalry regimental song. It had been adopted as the Seventh's song at the Battle of Washita.

It was during that first day that McIntosh was kicked by a horse, injuring his leg. The doctor ordered him back to the hospital at Fort Lincoln for a few days, so he and Mollie returned in an ambulance. The other officers' wives stayed on at camp.

Donald and Mollie McIntosh were back in camp within a few days. Custer threw on a buffalo hunt as entertainment before the regiment would leave for the Black Hills. The women went along, but were restricted in their role. When Mollie and Katie veered from the main hunt, a buffalo defending its young made a running attack on Mollie's horse, which was slowed down by a limp. Katie, who'd been getting shooting lessons from the officers at the garrison, shot the charging buffalo, but both women were scolded for leaving their designated spot amongst the main group of women.

As the date of departure for the Black Hills approached, the Custers decided to give a large picnic at camp, particularly for those women who had had to stay back at the forts to look after children. The families arrived aboard ambulances, buckboards, and wagons for the picnic and outdoor dance.

Preparations got down to details. The expedition was joined by a scientific party to study the geology, zoology, and paleontology of the hill area. Small pen and ink maps were made marking camp spots and streams, and the proposed Northern Pacific Railway. A company of Santee Sioux scouts — thirty-eight Sioux in addition to the twenty-two Arikara already accompanying the expedition — had come up from Nebraska to join Custer.

General orders of June 30 had established the "order of march." The Indian scouts would take the lead, followed by a battery of three Gatling guns and a cannon. Then came the ambulances and wagons, 110 in all, "the latter," according to orders, "when practicable to move in four columns." Next was an infantry battalion, marching in columns of two. Divided into two battalions, one company of the Seventh Cavalry would provide a rear guard while the other nine patrolled the expedition's flanks.[7]

The Seventh Cavalry heading out on the Plains for an expedition in 1874, two years before the battle of 1876.

At 4:20 a.m. on July 2, reveille sounded. Two soldiers waited outside each tent until the breakfast was over to begin packing up. Within two hours the breaking of camp was complete. "Boots and Saddle" sounded and the men saddled up. The Seventh Cavalry marched away, with more than one thousand men and one African-American woman, Aunt Sally as she was called, a cook. Vinatieri led the band playing "The Girl I Left Behind Me."

The women returned to the forts.

CHAPTER 16

THE SEVENTH CAVALRY AND THE BLACK HILLS

I T WAS SEVENTY YEARS AFTER THE LEWIS AND CLARK EXPEDI-
tion across the American northwest that Custer led his Seventh
Cavalry in virtually the same direction. The purpose of the Custer
1874 campaign into the Black Hills was three-fold: to find a route
to the west, look for suitable locations for forts, and investigate
the possibilities for gold mining in the area. This completely
ignored the Laramie Treaty of 1868 that protected the Native
rights in the area.

The expedition included a representative of the Corps of
Engineers and a number of scientists, including a geologist and
paleontologist. Their presence upheld the justification of science as
a reason for the trip, along with the research for sites for new military posts. Two mining experts were along, substantiating claims
that the real role was to invade Sioux territory in search of gold.

> [General] Terry who had been party to the 1868
> treaty negotiations, argued that duly authorized
> government officials had always been permitted
> entry upon the Sioux Reservation "in discharge of
> duties enjoined by law. I am unable to see that any
> just offense is given to the Indians by the expedition
> to the Black Hills."[1]

The party also included five correspondents representing newspapers in New York, Chicago, St. Paul, Minnesota, and Bismarck, the

Dakotas. And a St. Paul photographer, William H. Illingworth, was hired to record pictures of the exploration.

There were three Canadians on the Black Hills expedition. Lieutenant Donald McIntosh led Company G. In his diary he lists some accounts of supplies for the expedition. George Anderson was a trooper in Company K, led by Captain Owen Hale and Lieutenant Edward Godfrey. And Edmond Tessier was in Company L, led by Lieutenant Thomas Custer.

They left for the Black Hills on June 20 and proceeded at a pace set by Custer. He would often go out ahead with a few troops, sometimes as many as eighty men, exploring in one direction while sending others another way. This was more to Custer's liking. No longer did he have General Stanley to contend with. Custer was in charge and could roam at will. He sat astride his horse, in buckskins and a broad-brimmed hat set at a rakish angle on long reddish-blond hair. In the first few weeks there was little contact with Indians.

Those left back at Fort Abraham Lincoln and Fort Rice kept abreast of the expedition by means of letters carried by the so-called "Black Hills Express" — Indian scouts on ponies. In a letter dated July 2, 1874, Custer wrote to his wife Libbie from camp near Harney Peak, Dakota Territory.

> Breakfast at four. In the saddle at five....
>
> The expedition has surpassed most sanguine expectations. We have discovered a rich and beautiful country. We have had no Indian fights. We have found gold and probably other valuable metals. All are well. I did not expect my wagon train ... and here it has followed me all the way.[2]

Smoke signals dotted the skies along the horizons, alerting all the Natives to the presence of the enemy, but there was no outright attack. There were Indian sightings along the way, sometimes groups of twenty, sometimes fewer. The Sioux were at war with the Crow and Pawnee at the time. That may have been why they didn't engage the cavalry at some point during the expedition.

The expedition reached a cave referred to by the Indians as "Goose Cave." Custer said the walls were covered with drawings of animals and prints of hands and feet. Custer wrote to his wife on July 15, 1874, from a valley he named Prospect Valley.

> Captain Moylan who was in the rear on official duty saw about 25 following our trail. Signal smokes were sent up around us during the afternoon. Also Indians were seen watching us after we reached camp, but there were no hostile demonstrations. Some of the guides think the signals were to let their village know where we are, and to keep out of our way.
>
> We expect to reach the base of the Black Hills in about 3 days. Yesterday Prof. Winchel and Mr. Grinnell discovered the remains of an animal of an extinct race, larger than the largest size elephant.[3]

The regiment had to make nearly 300 miles before actually entering the Black Hills, and the ordered route was from Fort Lincoln to Bear Butte. The Seventh Cavalry arrived in the Black Hills on July 22 and set up a camp on the site of the future town of Custer. While the military searched for fort locations, the civilians in the expedition searched for gold. And on July 27 they found it — not a large amount, but enough to get excited about. Custer summoned his chief scout, "Lonesome" Charley Reynolds, and sent him out to report to his army superiors. Reynolds rode nights to fool the Indians. At Fort Laramie the word spread by telegraph, setting off another gold rush.

The Black Hills may have been all new to the white man, but they were familiar territory to the Native people. Any anticipated troubles did not materialize. On July 26, the expedition ran into the hunting party of Oglala Chief One Stab and his band of twenty-seven Sioux from the Red Cloud Agency in Nebraska. They were taken captive. Custer prevented his Arikara scouts from killing them, and the Sioux were later released unharmed.

By July 31, while Custer and a small party of explorers were climbing Harney's Peak five miles to the east, others of the expedition were enjoying themselves in another way.

> The big party was back at camp. The enlisted men whiled away the long summer day playing a game of baseball — a genuine Black Hills "first," including a dispute over the umpire's impartiality. Afterward, some of the cavalry officers hosted a champagne supper. A tarpaulin was spread under the pines, a box of cigars passed around, and bottles of champagne — at least one person, Illingworth's photograph shows — uncorked.[4]

For the first five days of August they were at Agnes Park, so named after a Custer family friend. Exploring parties fanned out to the south and southeast. It was near this camp that prospectors panning for gold had some luck. By August 15, they were at Bear Butte, Dakota Territory. Custer, an inveterate hunter, claimed he now had "the hunter's highest round of fame" — he had killed a grizzly bear.

The expedition had made its way all the way through the Black Hills. The entire party was astonished at the difference in topography, the change from the desert-like landscape to the knee-deep grasses and fresh water of the hill country. And gold had been discovered, no matter how unscientifically. It made newspaper headlines and started prospectors on their way to Dakota in further violation of the Sioux treaty rights.

The sixty-day campaign, 1,200 miles, ended with a flourish as the regimental band brought the Seventh back to Fort Abraham Lincoln to the sounds of "Garry Owen." The Illingworth photo shows the troops arriving home bedraggled but with an "unmistakable swagger of success."[5]

CHAPTER 17

MCINTOSH GOES SOUTH

During the two months that most of the Seventh Cavalry was in the field, the McIntosh household was dedicated to preparing for the wedding of Katie Garrett to Lieutenant Frank Gibson. The date was set for immediately following the return from the Black Hills expedition. In a portrait of pioneer women, and women in far-flung outposts, the officers' wives set to work sewing for the event. They gathered in the McIntosh living room, day after day, with Mollie in the lead. The Garrett girls' mother wouldn't be present, but had sent satin fabric from the east for the wedding gown. Mollie made orange blossoms from tufts of satin, using embroidery threads for the centres.

All the while they shared news from the letters sent back from the Hills. Letters full of wonders:

> The Belle Fourche yielded quantities of catfish which, though somewhat tasteless, made a change of diet at least. Bear Butte, the huge extinct volcano which faces Fort Meade today, was a thing of such stark, stupendous grandeur that it seemed almost like a mirage to the men accustomed to the stretches of desolate prairie, and the virgin soil surrounding this upheaval of countless ages ago was singularly fertile. Around the base of the mountain was discovered a quantity of exquisite pink marble, some of which in later years Lieutenant de Rudio

sculptured into delicate vases and other works of art for his quarters at Fort Meade[1]

Close to the date, the women from Fort Rice travelled to Lincoln for the wedding, and they brought the full-dress uniforms for their husbands, including the uniform for the groom. The men would have just hours to clean off weeks of whiskers and trail dust.

> The campaigners pulled into camp at dawn on August 30.... The day before, soldiers had swarmed all over the house downstairs, had hung a cotton wedding bell in the window of the living room, and had stretched white canvas over the floors of the parlor and dining room, while Mrs. Nash had darted up and down ladders, stringing bright colored cheesecloth draperies here and there.[2]

A punch of strong tea, laced with whiskey and citric acid, sat ready for the celebration. The wedding party dressed in the upstairs while officers and wives of the Seventh crowded into the downstairs. When Molly McIntosh began the wedding march on the piano, Katie descended the stairs.

> At the foot of the stairs Donald gave me his arm, and I walked the length of the living room toward the wedding bell, where the chaplain awaited us. On the right was my beloved, clean-shaved and as handsome as a god, while beside him was Captain Moylan, his best man. Then Frank took my hand, and we stood beneath the bell as Donald stepped a little away from me. Every time I glanced at him his smile and kind eyes braced me for the plunge.

When he gave me away, somehow his deep-toned,
positive voice assured me that all was well.[3]

Willie Cooke had returned from his six month's leave earlier in
the year on February 7, 1874. As regimental adjutant, he was posted
at Fort Abraham Lincoln in time for the wedding. Cooke joked afterwards that he had staged a full-dress parade in the bride's honour; a
parade everyone knew had been a regular inspection.

At Lincoln, on September 9, 1874, just ten days after the wedding,
Captain George Yates signed up the twenty-seven-year-old Canadian,
Sergeant Vickory, for another five-year stint, this time in Company F.
Vickory was chosen as regimental standard bearer.

That fall special order number 215 sent Major Lewis Merrill and
six companies of the Seventh to the department of the Gulf, companies assigned to different stations in Louisiana and Alabama. These
cavalry troops would be on security duties, really policing duties,
during the Reconstruction following the Civil War. There was still
a great deal of unrest in the South. They would be in place for more
than a year, until the spring of 1876.

Among the troops heading south were McIntosh in Company
G and Lieutenant Francis Gibson in Captain Frederick Benteen's
Company H.

On September 28, the contingent from Fort Rice travelled to Fort
Abraham Lincoln, bringing with it women and children destined for
the south as well. The McIntosh household provided beds for many.
Katie had a woman and two children in her room. Mrs. Benteen and a
child bunked in Mollie's. The men slept on makeshift tables throughout
the house. The troops and their families left Fort Abraham Lincoln by
train the next day, September 29, 1874. Mollie and Katie were heading
south. The two couples were able to make a stop in Washington, on the
way, to visit Mrs. Garrett.

The trip south was an easier trip than Katie had made four
months earlier. She described it as a "six-day picnic." The army was

everywhere in control of their journey, and there were no more bandit scares along the way. They all enjoyed the warm weather and abundance of fresh fruits and ice cream.

In Louisiana the troops were separated and sent to various locations. Company G, with McIntosh, was dispatched to Shreveport, arriving October 7, 1875. Company H, with Gibson, stayed at Jackson Barracks, New Orleans. This meant Mollie and Katie would be separated.

There was no room at the New Orleans camp for the wives and families, and so Katie found herself in a boarding house with another of the officers' wives. That stay was complicated by an epidemic of illness that Katie named the plague, but could have been some kind of influenza. The two women were quarantined for a time in an adjoining house while their boarding house was fumigated.

To add to the misery, Lieutenant Gibson found it difficult policing the increasing number of riots: "this duty is worse than Indian fighting because it is hard to prevent bloodshed among our own people." When both McIntosh's and Gibson's companies were called to Alabama, where disturbances had broken out, Mollie made a surprise visit to New Orleans to keep her sister company. For Katie this was a great relief:

> She [Mollie] was like a whiff of northern air to us all, and her visit did us lots of good. She was planning things to do every minute. She knew every card game under the sun, wielded a croquet mallet like a professional, played five musical instruments, and could tell a story better than anyone I ever heard.[4]

They stayed the winter of 1874–75 in the south. Then Gibson's company, Company A, was called to the west again. Frank Gibson returned to Fort Rice, but Katie stayed at Fort Abraham Lincoln until their Fort Rice house was ready. Then, for a while, she was alone at

Fort Rice while her husband was out at camp with the troops. Other companies were slowly making their way back to Fort Lincoln, but Donald and Mollie were still in the south with Company G.

Courtesy Little Bighorn Battlefield National Monument, #4844.

Lieutenant Donald McIntosh's dog, Shep, wearing a cavalry kepi (a French military-style hat) with a pipe in his mouth, 1875.

CHAPTER 18

MORE CANADIANS SIGN UP

I N THAT SPRING OF 1875, THE GOVERNMENT BROUGHT RED
Cloud and Spotted Tail back to Washington with the idea of
buying the Black Hills, which would end the Sioux hunting rights
along the Platte and Republican rivers. Back in the west, the chiefs
signed the document in June of 1875. They agreed to give up
hunting rights in the area wherever game was already depleted
anyway, but did not give up the Black Hills. This was another step
in further developing the Indians as wards of the government. And
by this time hundreds of whites were already in the Hills, settling
or hunting for gold.

In August, Washington sent a commission west to buy or lease
the Hills. Thousands of Natives gathered to hear the more aggressive Powder River bands deliver their answer — they didn't intend
to relinquish the Black Hills. A close friend of Crazy Horse, Little Big
Man, headed a band of 300 hostile warriors. Stripped and painted for
battle they chanted:

> Black Hills is my land and I love it
> And whoever interferes
> Will hear this gun[1]

The battle lines were drawn. It was clear that whatever the "agency
Sioux," those who lived off the government handouts, might decide,
Sitting Bull, Crazy Horse, and their people would fight to save their
culture and the Black Hills. The government offer, when it came, six

million dollars over a number of installments, was rejected by the Sioux. On November 3, 1875, President Grant secretly ordered that "no further resistance shall be made to miners going into [the Black Hills]." In his state of the Union message at the end of 1875, the president said that in the next year it would be increasingly difficult to protect Sioux treaty rights, and that the legislature would "have to adopt some measures to relieve the embarrassment" of the Black hills predicament.[2]

In June of 1875, the Canadian, Cooke, was commanding officer of Company F for seven weeks, but again he took holidays for a total of about three months. Back at Fort Abraham Lincoln on December 1, 1875, he was named post adjutant with special responsibilities for the scouts and the regimental band. In April of 1876, Cooke was relieved of his post as commander of scouts. Although he was primarily an adjutant, the various postings had given him some varied experience in the field.

A number of Canadians joined the Seventh Cavalry in 1875. They came from various parts of the country, from Upper Canada to Nova Scotia. There was a steady influx of these recruits, most in their twenties, from mid-summer through to late fall.

By the 1860s Yarmouth, Nova Scotia, had already celebrated its centennial and hit a population of 3,000. It was the second most important town in the province. Its industry centred on fishing, ship building, and commerce. There were foundries and factories, banks and hotels, and two weekly newspapers. The town did a great ship building business, and for its size, owned more shipping than any other port in the world. That gave it a view of the world that was more far-reaching than expected of a town of three-thousand.

The "California Fever" of 1849 stirred up much excitement in Yarmouth. A great crowd of about five hundred curious spectators gathered at Queen's wharf to watch as the sailing brigantine, "Mary Jane" left Yarmouth on November 22 to begin her long journey to San Francisco. After one hundred eighty-three days passage, she arrived at San Francisco on May 25, 1850. This was the first vessel to sail from a Nova Scotian port, for California district.[3]

And, during the American Civil War of the 1860s, Yarmouth forged another connection with the States.

"Yarmouth was a town almost on a war footing ... almost everybody was involved in [Yankee] blockade-running."

Union warships would do their best to keep supplies from entering southern ports, or cash crops from leaving, but the most trouble in the form of fast ships came from Nova Scotia and New Brunswick.

They operated out of Saint John ... They would buy materials from Boston factories, take them back to Saint John and then use a faster ship to take them from Saint John to some of the southern ports like Beaufort, Wilmington and Charleston.

"They were usually paid in English gold" ... Custer's men from Yarmouth heard so many stories of adventure that they likely couldn't resist looking for some of the action.[4]

Richard Saunders was the youngest son of Anthony and Aseneath Saunders, born in 1853 in Yarmouth County. A touch under six feet tall, Saunders had a dark complexion with brown hair and blue eyes. He worked locally as a stonemason. But maybe the sense of world adventure of a shipbuilding port, the closeness to the U.S. border, and stories of the local ships running the blockade during the Civil War, or all three, caused him to leave his home town. He made his way to Boston, Massachusetts, probably by steam ship. At a Boston recruiting station, Lieutenant William Harper Junior signed Saunders up to the Seventh Cavalry, Company D. It was August 16, 1875, and Richard D. Saunders was twenty-two years old.

James Harris was the other Yarmouth man to hear the call of the Seventh Cavalry. Twenty-one-year-old Harris was a house painter in the town. At the time of his enlistment he was described as having grey eyes and dark hair, but a fair complexion. He was five feet, six-and-a-half inches tall. Just over a month after Saunders, Harris signed up in Boston as well. Lieutenant Henry Lawton enlisted Harris as a private in Company D on September 21, 1875.

Nova Scotia gave up another of its sons to the United States Army in August of that year. James Weeks was born in Halifax in 1854, making him just twenty-one when he signed up. He had been working as a labourer and looked to the Seventh Cavalry as a way to get off that path. He was enlisted in Company M as a private by Lieutenant William Harper, Jr. in Boston on August 23.

Twenty-three-year-old Darwin L. Symms was already far from his home town when he joined the United States Army. Symms was born in Montreal, Canada East, now Quebec, in 1852. He was described as fair-haired, with blue eyes and fair complexion. His record shows he was five feet and nine inches tall. Symms had worked as a clerk, possibly in Chicago, which is where he signed his papers. Lieutenant Edmund Luff inducted Symms into the Seventh Cavalry, Company I. It was August 25, just a few days after Saunders and Weeks had joined, but in a different company.

Thomas Seayers was born in Canada West, now Ontario. He listed his hometown as Pikesville. By 1875, and at the age of twenty-one, Seayers had made his way to Cincinnati, Ohio. He may have been considered a little short in stature; his army record describes him as five feet, five-and-three-quarters-of-an-inch tall, with brown hair, brown eyes, and a dark complexion. It's probable that he was working as a baker in Cincinnati; he made his way to the United States Army recruiting office on September 10. Lieutenant Patrick Cusack signed him up to Company A. This company was in the south, and it's likely that Seayers joined it by train.

The next Canadian to sign up was a young carpenter, also from Montreal, John McShane. From Montreal it's a natural progression to New England and the city of Boston. Lieutenant Henry Lawton enlisted twenty-six-year-old McShane on September 20 at the Boston recruiting office, signing him onto the Seventh Cavalry, Company I. McShane had grey eyes, black hair, and a dark complexion. His height: just five feet, six inches tall.

Just days later, two more Canadians signed the papers to join the United States Army, each in a different location and different state.

Lieutenant-Colonel George Armstrong Custer and a hunting party in Dakota Territory, 1875. Elizabeth and George Custer are seated centre. Canadian William Winer Cooke is seated fourth from the right. Next to him, seated to the right, are Emma and Nellie Wadsworth and Thomas Custer.

Charles Orr was born in Paris, a small town in Canada West, now western Ontario. Paris sits on the banks of the Grand River not far from the U.S. border. Orr was born in 1847, just ten years after the Rebellion in Upper Canada later Ontario, a rebellion against the government that caught the interest of many Americans south of the border who actively participated, thinking Upper Canada would become another state of the union. Many participants freely fled across the border, south to safety, when the rebellion failed. So it wasn't unusual that someone from Paris would cross over, more than twenty years later, for a life in the United States.

Charles Orr was fair with blue eyes and nearly five feet, ten inches tall. By the age of twenty-eight, Orr was working as a painter in St. Louis. It was in St. Louis that he enlisted on September 24, 1875. Lieutenant John Thompson signed him up in the Seventh Cavalry, Company C.

The army records show Andrew Snow being born in Surrell, Canada, probably Sorel, Canada East. He had a ruddy complexion with hazel eyes and black hair, and he was the same height as Orr. Snow was a hostler, a person in charge of the stables usually at a hotel or inn, so he was a natural for the cavalry. Lieutenant Henry Lawton signed up twenty-two-year-old Snow on September 24, the same day as Orr was enlisting. Snow joined Company L.

The last Canadian to join Custer's cavalry that fall was Frank Myers. He was born in Canada East, in 1854. It was probably a rural area since Myers put his occupation as farmer at the time of his enlistment. He was another Canadian who had made his way to Cincinnati, Ohio, to enlist. Lieutenant Patrick Cusak signed him up as a private in the Seventh Cavalry, Company F. At twenty-one he was described as having grey eyes, brown hair, dark complexion, and stood just under five feet, nine inches. It was October 8, 1875.[5]

This is how the sixteen Canadians soldiers were sorted: Cooke was circulating in and out of companies, but most often was posted as an adjutant. McIntosh headed Company G. Myers had joined Vickory in Company F. Saunders and Harris were both in Company D. Tessier and Snow were both in Company L. Company I included McShane, Symms, and Hayward. Weeks was in Company M, and Orr in Company C. Anderson stayed in Company K. Seayers was in Company A. Another Canadian, MacAdams, was a lieutenant in the Second Cavalry in Montana, but was still destined to play a part at the Little Bighorn.

There was another Canadian, not a soldier, but a newspaper reporter, who also became involved with Custer and his next expedition in America's far northwest. He was Marcus (Mark) Henry Kellogg. Kellogg was born in Brighton, Upper Canada, on the shores of Lake Ontario in 1833. His parents, Simon and Lorenda Whelpley Kellogg, had migrated from Vermont to Upper Canada. They settled in the village of Brighton, situated about halfway between York (now Toronto) and Montreal. This meant Kellogg had dual citizenship, Canadian-American.

Brighton had been settled by United Empire Loyalists crossing the border about forty years earlier. At the time the Kelloggs lived in the village, the population was near 500, the average farm was 100 acres — the apple orchards of the future were in their beginnings.

But the Kellogg family didn't stay in one spot long, moving around Canada a number of times before settling south of the border in La Crosse, Wisconsin, in 1851, when Mark Kellogg was eighteen. The elder Kellogg operated the Western Enterprise Hotel, which he bought and renamed the Kellogg House Hotel. Mark worked as his clerk. He left his father's employ and worked for a time as a telegrapher. But in the 1860s Kellogg got his first job with a newspaper, working as a cashier for *The Democrat* owned by M.M. "Brick" Pomeroy. In May of 1861 he married Martha L. Robinson. They had two children, daughters Cora Sue and Martha Grace.

In 1867, Kellogg not only played shortstop on one of the town's baseball teams, he also dipped his toe into politics, getting the Democratic Party nod as candidate for city clerk of La Crosse.

Kellogg was defeated. He lost the election in April; he lost his wife in May. Six years to the day that he had married Martha Robinson, he buried her. Some time in the next months, Kellogg left his daughters of five and two years with their grand-parents, Charles and Hannah Robinson, and then he left La Crosse.[6]

Pomeroy also owned *The Democrat* in Council Bluffs, Iowa, and Kellogg's move as assistant editor for *The Democrat* there continued to have political overtones. A one-time supporter of the local campaign for Republican Abraham Lincoln, he was now a member of a radical version of the Democrats known as Copperheads. Copperheads either sympathized with the South in the Civil War to a high degree or disagreed with the war itself. They were also known as "red hot" Democrats. The owner, Pomeroy, sent out radical flyers accusing the government of wanting to hold the white South in eternal bondage. Kellogg's departure from *The Democrat* in Council Bluffs, Iowa, in 1868 was not a pleasant one.

Resentment informed Kellogg's assertion of having gone without "a cent of remuneration, or an exhi-bition of appreciation in any shape whatever," his efforts in behalf of the community notwithstand-ing. Having *"starved nearly to death,"* he reserved his thanks for the *"few"* who had shown kindness.[7]

Kellogg apparently returned to La Crosse, Wisconsin, and his family, working as a printer. He joined the girls living with the maternal grandparents in a large house that also had boarders. Kellogg was not considered a striking man in demeanor; described as an "unprepossessing, little-known and self-effacing part-time journalist."[8] A quiet face distinguished by a prominent, bony nose, his dark hair was short but not militarily short, and sideburns found their way to his chin. He may have been unprepossessing, but certainly he was adventurous. On the move again he spent some time in Brainerd, Minnesota, where he ran for election to the legislature, but again went down in defeat.

His roaming continued, and he worked as a telegraphic operator during the 1870–73 construction of the Northern Pacific Railway, following the line as it progressed from Duluth to Bismarck. He showed up in Bismarck, North Dakota, right across the river from Fort Abraham Lincoln, in 1873. There, he became editorial assistant on *The Bismarck Tribune.*

During this period he was also a correspondent for the St. Paul and Minneapolis *Pioneer-Press and Tribune,* writing under the nom de plume of "Frontier." According to the paper, Kellogg was deemed to have a "bold and adventurous spirit" and was "greatly fascinated with frontier life." He seemed to have adopted a pioneer mood as intense as his former Democratic Party one. On July 10, 1875, he wrote angrily from Bismarck of the killing of a homesteader by an Indian raiding party just three miles from Fort Abraham Lincoln. An article that was published in the paper on August 18:

And thus they go, making raids here and there, killing inoffensive white citizens, raiding off stock, and doing pretty much as they please, with utmost impunity — and yet the present Indian policy calls out for 'Peace! Peace! — christianize [*sic*] the poor unfortunates, treat them with kindness,' and all that bosh. Bah! I say, turn the dogs of war loose, and drive them off the face of the earth, if they do not behave themselves.[9]

CHAPTER 19

THE HODGSON INCIDENT

Donald and Mollie McIntosh stayed in Shreveport, Louisiana, until well into 1876.

The troops were recalled to the Department of the Dakota. And it was in April that some incidents occurred, involving Lieutenant McIntosh in a disciplinary battle with another officer, Second Lieutenant Benjamin Hodgson of Company B. The troops had left St. Louis, Missouri, by train Saturday, April 22, on the way to St. Paul, Minnesota. They arrived in Ottumwa, Iowa, on Sunday and spent a couple of hours there. The stock car had run off the track, and the tender broke down delaying the train. They arrived in Austin, Minnesota, on Monday the 25th at about 11 p.m. and left three and a half hours later.

During this period there were a couple of incidents involving Second Lieutenant Hodgson and Lieutenant Donald McIntosh. The letter that McIntosh wrote to his superiors later indicates the first incident had occurred in St. Louis, presumably just before or while leaving that city. Second Lieutenant Hodgson, known as Benny, was often described as "diminutive," irrepressible, and well-liked by everyone, but he obviously had his troubling moments. He was apparently on the brink of shooting a soldier in anger when McIntosh stepped in and prevented him. Then on the train, enroute from St. Louis to Austin, a quarrel broke out between the two men.

In his diary, McIntosh noted that at midnight on April 25 he placed Hodgson under arrest. It's not clear why he hadn't arrested

Hodgson in St. Louis on Friday, April 21, or Saturday, April 22, when Hodgson was involved in the attempted shooting incident.

On April 25, there were two rail accidents — the stock car ran off the tracks and an engine broke down, causing a delay of many hours. They weren't able to leave until 2:30 in the morning. It was during this time the second offence occurred. It involved back-talk to McIntosh, a superior officer, and that may have been seen as a more serious offence than threatening to shoot someone, as far as McIntosh was concerned. At any rate, on April 25, McIntosh, as senior officer, placed Hodgson under arrest after the second incident.

McIntosh states his case in a letter to headquarters in St. Paul:

Det. Troops B & G 7th Cav

On the cars (train) en route from Shreveport to St. Paul

Respectfully forwarded

These are the facts of the case, briefly, according to my recollection.

On the occasion referred to the confuct [sic] of [Second] Lt. Hodgson was, at first, rude. I said to him I wished to discuss no nonsense or hear any impertinence. His conduct then became, in my judgment, aggravating, disrespectful and contemptuous. I then told him he had better behave himself, whereupon he became defiant both in manner and speech. I placed him in arrest, which, of course, suspended his official functions, and his troop [B] was put under the command of Lieut. [George] Wallace.

This is not the first instance of the kind since leaving the Dept. of the South. While preventing

him from committing an act of violence against an
enlisted man of his company, at St. Louis, [shoot-
ing him] he rudely pushed me aside accompanying
the act with very improper language. This in the
presence of his whole company. I also regret to say
that this line of conduct on the part of Lt. Hodgson
did not cease with his arrest.[1]

When they arrived in St. Paul, Minnesota, Hodgson answered
with his own letter to the adjutant-general, headquarters of the
Department of Dakota, giving his side of the story. It was dated
April 25, 1876.

Sir:

Have the honor to request your attention to the
following.

On yesterday 24th, at Austin, Min, while en route
to this point, I was placed in arrest and deprived
of command of my company by 1st Lt McIntosh
Comdg. Det. 7th Cavy.

I desire respectfully to invite the attention
of the commanding general to this action of Lt.
McIntosh, and without entering into any discussion here, I will say, thus officially, and with
thorough appreciation of the fact that I may be
required under penalties to substantiate the statement — that Lt., McIntosh had no provocation,
cause, reasons or excuse for his proceedings, which
I regard as an arbitrary, unjust and tyrannical
attempt to humiliate me. I regard it as a grievance
second to none which could be inflicted on me in
my official capacity, and I beg the Comdg Genl to

discountenance it right — meanwhile should I in his opinion, be in the wrong I ask no indulgence, no relaxation of the law and penalties covering such cases.

I am, Sir
Very respectfully
Your Ob Sevt
B.H. Hodgson
2nd Lt. 7th Cavy [2]

While not a running commentary on the days' happenings, McIntosh's diary, which he carried with him throughout his cavalry service, does reflect some of the dynamics of McIntosh's life at the time. It sets out a back-and-forth cribbage competition between McIntosh and Lieutenant Edward S. Godfrey, with Godfrey the overall champ — and notes that Lieutenant Hodgson withdrew himself from the mess, paying a mess bill of $12.

CHAPTER 20

THE BLACK HILLS STRATEGY

CUSTER AND HIS WIFE, ELIZABETH, SPENT PART OF THE WINTER of 1875 in New York City. They made up a party, sometimes including Custer's brother Tom and Willie Cooke. The Custers considered Cooke one of their closest friends. They all spent the days and nights at the theatre and enjoying the social scene.

At the same time Custer was keeping an eye on the army, and his own career, and even considering a speaking tour request. In January of 1876, he wrote from New York to his brother Tom:

> The latest in regard to Army reduction is that the House will not interfere with the Cavalry, but will cut off 5 regiments of Infantry, and one of Artillery.
>
> I have no idea of obtaining my promotion this spring or summer. On the contrary. I expect to be in the field, in the summer, with the 7th, and think there will be lively work before us. I think the 7th Cavalry may have its greatest campaign ahead....
>
> Mr. Pond, manager of the Redpath Agency [in Boston] has come to see me and offer a contract. When I tell you the terms you will open your eyes. Five nights a week for from four to five months, I to receive $200 a night ... They urge me to commence this spring, but I declined, needing more time for preparation.[1]

On return to Fort Abraham Lincoln in mid-winter, Custer was ordered back east, to Washington, where he was involved in a number of hearings into army affairs over a period of weeks that spring. He also testified against President Grant's secretary of war, William Belknap. Belknap was accused of accepting bribes. One specific case stated he received $24,450 for awarding the Fort Sill sutler's rights to John Evans. Belknap's wife was also thought to be involved. Belknap was impeached in the House of Representatives but, having been warned, he resigned before action could be taken against him.

A sutler was the general storekeeper on an army post. Six years earlier this post had become an appointment through the secretary of War, and often subject to purchase by bribery. These traders then sold goods including weapons, the newest and the best, often to hostile Indians who would use them against the soldiers. For example, in February of 1874, sutler John E. Smith wrote to Custer regarding Indian activity north of the Platte and west of the Missouri rivers.

> Fully half the young men have pistols — one or more, exclusive of other arms. About half the warriors remaining at Agencies have repeating rifles, Winchesters & all others have breech-loaders. I have known Indians at White River Agency to have 3,000 rounds of ammunition for a single gun.[2]

While in Washington, Custer attended all the best parties, writing back to his wife at Fort Lincoln in April details of the dinner parties and how "well received" he was. Washington newspapers took sides on the Custer factor in all the various army hearings, some for, some against. During this time Custer also let it be known that he did not think much of President Grant's brother Orvil, who may also have taken bribes.

By April 23, 1876, Custer had made his escape from the capital, on his way back west, and got as far as New York City. He stayed there making the social rounds, as usual, and bragging about them in letters to his wife. But a few days later was stopped in his tracks. He was ordered back to the capital for more testimony. On April 28, he wrote to Libbie of his appearance at the Impeachment Board which continued hearings despite Belknap's resignation.

> I send you a newspaper describing my dress as I sat with Representatives Clymer, Blackburn & Robbins of the Impeachment Board. It states that "Genl. Custer wore black coat and light pants" — Both Tom's — and "white vest." Tell Tom I intend to charge him for having his clothes advertised....
>
> Do not be anxious. I seek to follow a moderate and prudent course, avoiding prominence. Nevertheless, everything I do, however simple and unimportant, is noticed and commented on. This only makes me more careful.[3]

But not careful enough as it turned out. Once again Custer set out by train for Dakota Territory only to be met at Chicago by an officer with orders to detain him "on grounds he had left the national capital without paying his obligatory calls on General Sherman and the president." Custer's animosity toward the president's brother, and his testimony against Secretary of War Belknap, did not make him popular with the president. Grant, personally incorruptible but quite touchy, had retaliated.

Custer put up his defence by telegram, stating that he had tried but failed to meet with the two men in question. But the biggest blow came when he got to St. Paul, Minnesota. At army headquarters there he found that President Grant had forbade him from joining the upcoming expedition against the Sioux. It would be led by General Terry.

A humble Custer, with the help of Terry, sent a telegram to the president.

As my entire regiment forms a part of the proposed expedition, and as I am the senior officer of the regiment on duty in this Department, I respectfully but most earnestly request that while not allowed to go in command of the expedition, I may be permitted to serve with my regiment in the field.

I appeal to you as a soldier to spare me the humiliation of seeing my regiment march to meet the enemy and I not share in its dangers.[4]

A quick exchange of letters in May involving General Sheridan followed. The issue was resolved with a telegraph from General Sherman to General Terry.

The dispatch of General Sheridan enclosing yours of yesterday touching General Custer's urgent request to go under your command with his regiment, has been submitted to the President who sends me word that if you want General Custer along he withdraws his objections. Advise Custer to be prudent not to take along any newspaper men who always work mischief, and to abstain from any personalities in the future. Tell him I want him to confine his whole mind to his legitimate office. ... [5]

On May 10, Custer arrived back at Fort Lincoln, having been away for seven weeks.

The situation in the west, where settlers and those seeking gold were being attacked by Natives, had become more and more a concern for the government. By late 1875, Washington decided to take action on the Indian unrest. The president authorized the War Department to show the warlike tribes that this behaviour couldn't continue.

And by 1876, General Sheridan had drawn up a plan. Three armies would converge on the Black Hills area. General George Crook would move north from Fort Fetterman in eastern Wyoming. Colonel John Gibbon would move east from Montana. General Alfred Terry, with Custer in command of the Seventh, would move west from Dakota Territory. In fact, what this did was drive a number of Indian tribes from their villages, consolidating a number of them with the Crazy Horse–Sitting Bull camps.

In February of 1876, it was estimated that 15,000 miners had flooded into the Hills. And outlaws had arrived as well. Wild Bill Hickok and Calamity Jane were already working the area. Butch Cassidy and his gang robbed their first bank in Belle Fourche, just north of the Hills. The military began preparations for action against the Sioux.

It had been a severe winter, and by early spring Cheyenne and other Sioux were streaming toward the Powder River for the spring hunt. They gathered along the banks of the Rosebud River, about 15,000 or more Sioux moving northward in search of game. Early in June the Sioux held their annual Sun Dance where Sitting Bull dreamed of white soldiers falling dead in his camp.

Meanwhile, the government still believed there were only about 500 off-reservation Sioux in the area, as had been reported the previous year.

In March of 1876, General George Crook headed out to round up some Sioux in southeastern Montana. At one time Crook had been considered by the Indians as a white leader whom they could trust to keep his word. But now his mission for the army was to wage war. A year earlier he was asked if it was not hard to go on another Indian campaign to which he made the famous answer, "Yes, it is hard. But, sir, the hardest thing is to go and fight those whom you know are in the right."[6]

An advance party led by Colonel J.J. Reynolds attacked a village, thinking it belonged to Crazy Horse, and set it on fire. Teepees stuffed with ammunition exploded. Reynolds panicked, leaving behind three dead troopers and one wounded soldier. Reynolds was later court-martialled. The refugees from the village went on to join Crazy Horse and Sitting Bull.[7]

These Cheyenes, Oglalas, and Unkpapas drifted north-westerly, gathering strength from other tribes as they travelled.

General Crook reorganized at Fort Fetterman, and, on May 29, started north again. He received a courier report "that all able-bodied male Indians had left the Red Cloud Agency." It was the time of year that the Indians would leave the agencies, or treaty areas, for the non-treaty camps, and he wanted to find the village before it was reinforced by these treaty warriors.[8]

The third week of June, on June 17, Crook ran into about 1,000 Indians. His soldiers fought a six-hour battle against Crazy Horse's warriors on the banks of the Rosebud. Crook's forces finally retreated to his supply base. He lost nine troopers, and the Natives lost about forty warriors. The Sioux then moved west along the Little Big Horn River where they found antelope and sweeping pastures for their horses.

Meanwhile, Colonel Gibbon assembled his troops from three different forts and a field camp. The idea was that he would meet Colonel Terry and Custer along the Yellowstone River, above the Sioux, while Crook would threaten them from the south. Colonel Gibbon set out in March, heading south to the Yellowstone River, then eastward.[9]

Gibbon was months on the move. The Montana Column wound eastward in a leisurely manner with only a few run-ins with the Indians. The Canadian, Lieutenant MacAdams, of the Second Cavalry, rode in that column.

CHAPTER 21

JOURNALIST MARK KELLOGG

I N MAY, THE SEVENTH CAVALRY SET UP CAMP ABOUT TWELVE miles down the valley from Fort Abraham Lincoln in prepara-tion for General Terry's expedition. The wagon train left the fort in a foggy dawn with more than 150 packed wagons, with infantry and an artillery detachment of four guns as escort.

Terry and Custer decided a show would be the best policy for the main leave-taking, and by 7:00 on the morning of May 17, 1876, the troops marched around the parade square led by Custer, his regi-mental staff, Libbie, his sister, Maggie (Mrs. James Calhoun), and a cousin, Emma Reed. Vinatieri and the band came next, mounted on white horses, playing "Garry Owen." They circled Laundry Row, so called because many of the troopers' wives did laundry at the fort. Children waved flags and women cried. Once outside the fort, Donald McIntosh and the other married officers dismounted; Donald to say goodbye to his beloved Mollie, and the other officers to say farewell to their wives and families.

The column stretched two miles and was comprised of the cavalry, artillery, infantry, ponies, pack mules, scouts, and civil-ians — 1,200 men and 1,700 animals. At the very front rode Col. Custer, beside him his wife, Libbie. Vinatieri and the regimental band struck up "The Girl I Left Behind Me."

> If ever I get off the trail and the Indians don't find me
> I'll make my way straight back to the girl I left
> behind me

That sweet little girl, that true little girl,
The girl I left behind me[1]

The column stayed in camp that night, May 17. The paymaster was on hand to settle the men's pay and accounts. The next day he escorted Elizabeth Custer, her sister-in-law Maggie, and Emma Reed back to Fort Lincoln.

In the expedition there was a collection of whites and Indians hired as scouts, including thirty Arikaras and four Lakota Sioux. Bloody Knife, half-Arikara and half-Sioux, was a Custer favourite. Prior to setting out, Custer gave him a medal he had from Washington and a black handkerchief spotted with stars. Raised by the Sioux, Bloody Knife had been bullied in his youth because of his Arikara heritage, particularly by a Sioux boy named Gall. He had taken some revenge years earlier by leading an army raid on Gall's camp, which left Gall for dead. Gall had survived, and Bloody Knife looked forward to finding the hostile camp and meeting up with him once more.

Another important scout was "Lonesome" Charley Reynolds, considered the best white guide in Dakota Territory. He had already reported to Custer that the Lakota Sioux under Sitting Bull were gathering in force. He said they were preparing for war by collecting Winchester repeating rifles, and plenty of ammunition.[2]

The column of the Seventh had twelve companies. Custer divided his column into two wings. Each wing had two battalions, and each battalion had three companies. Major Marcus Reno led the right wing, Captain Frederick Benteen headed up the left. Neither one of these leaders was a member of Custer's inner circle; they didn't even like him. And they weren't friendly with each other, either.

Reno's reputation suffered through his heavy drinking. He had been acting commanding officer of the Seventh Cavalry, standing in for Custer who was away in the east during the winter and spring;

Custer hadn't been satisfied with the regiment's preparation for the expedition. And the major lacked any real Indian fighting experience.

The regiment had not fought anyone in the past three years, and four companies had not been in combat in seven years, having been assigned to chasing the Ku Klux Klan and moonshiners in the south. The previous year, 150 new men had enlisted, including nine of the fifteen Canadian troopers. (MacAdams was with the Second Infantry in Colonel Gibbon's Montana Column and Kellogg was a journalist.) Only 30 percent had ever fought Indians. All twelve of the companies had never served together before. "The overall caliber of the Army's enlisted ranks had deteriorated noticeably since the end of the Civil war. In the Seventh Cavalry alone, more than ten percent of the men had enlisted under an alias."[3]

The composition of the Custer Column included all the Canadians in the cavalry, except Hayward and Anderson, plus journalist Mark Kellogg. At forty-three years old, Kellogg was beginning to gray and wore steel-rimmed glasses. He was included because of an unexpected occurrence. Although the Washington edict had clearly stated there should be no newspaper men along, Custer had invited the editor of the Bismarck Tribune, Clement A. Lounsberry, to accompany him. When Lounsberry heard that a military column including the Seventh Cavalry commanded by Lieutenant-Colonel Custer was heading for Montana Territory, he agreed to go along and provide newspaper coverage. At the last minute he had to abandon the trip when his wife fell ill. Lounsberry asked his assistant, Kellogg, to take his place as correspondent. He gave Kellogg his military belt still bearing the blackened stains of Lounsberry's blood, shed in his Civil War service with Custer.

Known to the army scouts as "The-Man-Who-Makes-Paper-Talk," Kellogg became an object of amusement to the troopers on the expedition, as he kept up with the larger cavalry mounts on a little grey mule from whose back his toes could touch the ground. "Kellogg travelled light. He was unarmed and kept his writing materials in a black satchel along with tobacco and pipes."[4]

Kellogg kept a running diary, which he entitled "Notes of the Little Big Horn Expedition under General Custer, 1876." These were not military notes but more travelogue entries, often make striking comments. Kellogg began with the departure from Fort Lincoln. He wrote the notes in pencil, in a book he kept with him.

> May 17th — Broke camp early morning, foggy, heavy roads. Forming marching order two miles west Ft. Lincoln. Camped at 3 p.m. on the Big Heart, 13 ½ miles traveled. Splendid camp, wood, grass and water plenty.
> May 18th — Reveille 3 a.m. Under march 5 a.m. Halted at noon on Sweet Brier, 10 5/8 miles traveled. Slight rains near camp, heavy rains all round. In camp at 4 p.m. Custer in person; energy.[5]

He noted that Custer and Terry rode out ahead of the troops with a couple of companies over the next couple of days. Heavy rains made the going rough. Within four days they approached the Bad Lands, buttes with what Kellogg calls "peculiar names" like Rattlesnake, Wolfe's Den, and Maiden's Breasts. The army veterinary surgeon took up his duties as soon as they made camp, tending to the animals. Reynolds was out in the early morning hours before daylight; found one of the trails from the Pacific Northwest railway expedition three years earlier.

> May 22nd — Reveille 3 a.m. Broke camp 6 a.m. Column took up line of march; weather, clear, cool and pleasant. Getting beyond water shed,

roads harder, drier. Was at front with Terry and Custer all day; but little scouting done today. The guides, Reynolds and Bloody Knife, ahead. Plenty of antelope seen today. Reynolds killed three, and fourteen in all were brought in. Struck Custer's return Black Hills trail of '74 at 10 a.m.[6]

By May 28, the column had left the grassy plains of the prairie and entered the Little Missouri River Badlands. They now faced deep canyons and few trees. They were making up to nineteen miles a day. Mail carriers and couriers travelled between them and Fort Lincoln. Though in Indian country there was little evidence of Indians so far. There seemed to be no fear of the warriors, just a push to catch them before they scattered. In the first week of June, they reached the Powder River without having seen any Indians.

May 24.... General Custer, Captain Tom Custer and party miles away on right flank hunting nearly most of day; killed elk and lynx. Crossed line of survey of Northern Pacific Railroad at 9 a.m.... Face of country past two days, high rolling prairie, very beautiful in its green carpet. On cut bank of stream, opposite camp (fork of Big Heart River), is a plainly defined stratum of lignite, five to six feet in depth....[7]

Toward the end of May they were entering the Badlands. Kellogg noted that General Terry was out in front all day "pioneering" the trail. Terry laid all the camps and attended in person to much of the march detail. "Past two days we have marched between the Stanley trail west of '73 and Custer's return Yellowstone trail of '73; it is excellent route thus far; should properly be called Terry's trail."[8] And every day Vinatieri struck up the band as the column hit the trail, playing again in the evening at camp.

Custer had a number of relatives and friends aboard the expedition, including his young brother, Boston. On June 8, Boston wrote to his mother from camp about twenty miles from the mouth of the Powder River, Montana Territory.

> We are the first white men to visit the river at this place. We and the command marched here yesterday, traveling thirty-two miles. We found some country you would call rather rough. Armstrong [Custer], Tom, Col Cook [Lieutenant William Cooke], myself and Lt. Edgerly with his detail with a few Indian guides, rode ahead of the column, to find a road....
>
> I am feeling first-rate and joke Tom and Mr. Cook about their being tired by the ride to camp, for, as soon as a fire was built, they both stretched out for a sleep ... I don't think we will get back to Lincoln before September, but that will suit me. I would rather be here than in garrison....
>
> Sometimes she [his sister Maggie] cuffs my ears, saying that if you did so when I was a child it is perfectly right for her to do so now....[9]

While the Seventh was making its way west, General John Gibbon and the Montana Column had been operating along the Yellowstone River for more than a month, heading east from Fort Ellis. This column had five companies of infantry and four of cavalry, including Lieutenant MacAdams of the Second Cavalry.

By the end of May, Gibbon's troops had spied a large gathering of Natives on the Rosebud River, almost 500 lodges. Gibbon didn't attack, possibly because the village had twice as many Indians as his 400 men. In his message to Terry he seemed to downplay this sighting, mentioning it only slightly in a postscript. "P.S. A camp some distance up the Rosebud was reported this morning by our scouts. If this proves true, I may not start down the Yellowstone so soon."[10]

Courtesy of Sandy Barnard.

A portrait of journalist Mark Kellogg, probably taken between 1863 and 1865. Kellogg was born in Brighton, Upper Canada, now Ontario.

In the continuing pincer movement against the Indians, General Crook moved north, bolstered by the addition of sixty-five "discouraged miners" and 260 Crow and Shoshone scouts, longtime enemies of the Sioux. Mid-June, Crook left his wagon train under guard and with about 1,300 men began a march to find the Indians. Topping Custer, Crook had five newspapermen with his column. The Indians on the Rosebud River, hearing of this activity "packed up their tepees and moved west over the divide into the valley of the Little Bighorn River on June 15."[11]

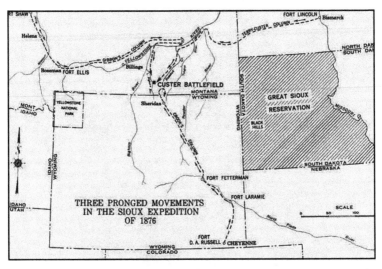

The three U.S. Army generals led their columns in a pincer movement against the Sioux in the expedition of 1876.

CHAPTER 22

THE MARCH WEST

MID-JUNE, ABOUT FIFTY MILES SOUTH OF THE YELLOWSTONE River, a sacred Lakota Sioux ceremony took place. It was held every summer to purify and strengthen the tribes and test the dedication of the young warriors. It lasted several days, and only Hunkpapas participated this time. The young endured various ordeals while older men, through self-torture, hoped to induce visions from the gods. Forty-five year old Sitting Bull was among them. His hands and feet were stained red, his shoulders crossed with blue stripes. He sat on the ground while his adopted brother, Jumping Bull, made fifty cuts on his arms. Then he danced. Sitting Bull seemed unaware of blood trickling down his arms. He danced for hours and sank into a trance. When revived he talked about a dream in which the Sioux killed enemy soldiers.[1]

> Sitting Bull's village — by now consisting of virtually every Cheyenne and Lakota nontreaty band — derived even more confidence and strength from his prophecy. With the conclusion of the Sun Dance, they continued up the Rosebud, then decided to follow the buffalo herds that their scouts had sighted to the west, in the valley of the Greasy Grass, the river the whites called Little Bighorn.[2]

At this parallel, rivers run north, so the Indians were going south as they headed "up the Rosebud."

Custer's column was making as much as thirty-two miles some days according to Kellogg. On June 7, he noted that Company D, including the Canadians Saunders and Harris, acted as a scouting party helping to find a trail forward. His admiration for Custer comes through in his abbreviated notes.

General Custer with Colonel Weir's troop used as vedettes, scouted ahead and succeeded in finding a passable trail route over a country which would seem impracticable — up, down, zigzag, twirling, turning, and General Custer rode fifty miles; fresh when arrived. Told Terry last evening would succeed in finding trail and water horse in Powder river [*sic*] at 3 p.m. today; succeeded at 3:30 p.m. Most attractive scenery yet; spruce and cedar on buttes; marched on "Hogs Back," highest buttes in country for mile or two; if teams went either side would roll down hundreds of feet.[3]

The next day General Terry with two companies left for the mouth of the Powder River to intercept the steamer *Far West*. Kellogg also reported that scouts from General Gibbon's column, who had met with Custer, had been sent back to Gibbon with messages from Terry. But driven back by hostile Indians, they were unable to reach the Montana column.

June 9th — Lay in camp today. Scouts came in from mouth of Powder river with mail brought up by steamer *Far West* and information that General Terry had gone up Yellowstone river thirty miles on steamer. Meet Gibbon, who, marching down Yellowstone river valley, forms junction with Terry. Organization for scouting completed and only

awaits General Terry's return. It is probable the
bulk of hostiles are on Tongue river and between
trail and Powder river.[4]

General Crook's column was camped a few miles from Rosebud
Creek, and on the morning of June 17 it headed out. After about an
hour Crook called a halt. Scouts were sent on ahead. Meanwhile Sitting
Bull's warriors were painted and dressed for battle. When Crook's scouts
returned to camp the warriors followed them making a quick attack.
In the ravines and hills the battle raged for six hours — Crook's 1,300
men against the 700 warriors. When the Indians finally retreated north
through narrow canyons, to draw the solders in, Crook's scouts argued
against following them since the narrow confines were too dangerous.

General Crook had gone on the trek north without his pack
train, with its supplies and extra ammunition. After the fight, he
turned back south to Goose Creek and sent the dead and wounded
back to Fort Fetterman. Crook kept his men at Goose Creek for the
next six week awaiting supplies.

News of the battle, the size of the Indian fighting force, and the
virtual defeat of the troops, didn't reach General Sheridan in Chicago
until June 23. Crook never did alert Terry or Gibbon about the large
numbers of Indians nearby at the Rosebud River. Crook had not
been able to conquer the Indians with his 1,300 men, and Terry had
only 700. The strongest force of the three-pronged pincer movement
was out of action, and Sheridan had counted on all three.

Meanwhile, Colonel Gibbon's command from Montana was moving
into position to join up with Terry and Custer. The government char-
tered steamers, *Far West* and *Josephine*, were providing supplies to a
depot where the Glendive Creek meets the Yellowstone River. The
Far West then received orders from Terry to establish a depot further
along the Yellowstone, at the mouth of the Powder River.

After a meeting with Gibbon and still with no certainty where the Indian encampment was located — he had heard nothing from Crook — Terry decided he needed a reconnaissance to find the Indian village with the non-treaty Indians. He chose Major Reno for the assignment, not Custer. Major Reno was ordered to take the six companies of the right wing. He would do a circular tour — up the Powder River (travelling south), crossing west to the Tongue River and down the Tongue (travelling north) to the Yellowstone — meeting up again with the Dakota column.

At least eight Canadians went with him. Sergeant John Vickory was on duty with Captain George Yates and Company F, along with Frank Myers. John McShane, Darwin Symms, and George Hayward, the saddler, were in Company I, led by Captain Myles Keogh. Edmund Tessier and Andrew Snow were in Company L, led by Lieutenant James Calhoun, and Charles Orr was in Company C under Captain Tom Custer; both companies assigned to Reno.

After two or three days hard going Reno reached the Tongue where he found evidence of about 400 Indian lodges. After about a week he strayed from Terry's orders and took his command further west to Rosebud Creek. There he found signs again of Indian encampment, and on June 17 — the very day Crook and the Indians were engaged in battle — Reno found signs of the villages moving south, upstream in the Rosebud Valley.

Realizing he was in no position to fight with his small and weary command, Reno turned north down the Rosebud to the Yellowstone River, then east to the rendezvous with Terry at the Tongue.

The day after Reno and the right wing had left on the reconnaissance, on June 11, Custer took his remaining troops to the supply depot on the Yellowstone River. The *Far West* arrived, and Custer was disappointed to find his wife, Libbie, was not on board as they had planned.

Custer wrote to Elizabeth on June 11, 1876, from the mouth of the Powder River, Montana Territory. General Terry was concerned the supply wagons wouldn't get through to the mouth of the Powder River, because of the heavy terrain.

> He had ridden to the mouth of the Powder and he and those with him had expressed a fear that the wagons would not make it in a month, on account of the intervening Bad Lands. He came to my tent early this morning and asked if I would try to find a road ... The men had only rations for one day left. One company had been sent out the day before, but had not returned. Sure enough we found them. We have all arrived here safely and the wagons besides.[5]

Four days later Custer took the six companies of the left wing along the south shore of the Yellowstone to the Tongue to meet Reno. The *Far West* followed, but not the band. Felix Vinatieri and the band were left at the Powder River camp. The band's white horses were taken as transport for some of the un-mounted troopers. About 150 of the new recruits were left behind. The regiment's sabres were boxed up and left as well.

General Terry had misgivings about Reno's actions in not following orders and possibly alerting the Indians to his position. On the other hand, Reno was also criticized because he didn't seek battle, although he was out-numbered. From the camp in Powder River Valley, Custer wrote to his wife Elizabeth:

> [Reno's] scouting party has returned. I fear their failure to follow up the trails has imperiled our plans by giving the village an intimation of our presence. Think of the valuable time lost.[6]

The entire command moved to the junction of the Rosebud and the Yellowstone. Terry had set up his command on the *Far West* and, on the night of June 21, the senior officers met aboard the steamer to plan the attack. Willie Cook and Donald McIntosh were among them. The military expected the Indians to move south since they were already aware of Gibbon's Montana column and Terry's Dakota command being in the area. Custer, Terry, and Gibbon counted on Crook coming up from the south. None of them knew that Crook had already met the Sioux and been forced to retreat. Their plan was still a three-pronged pincer that would catch the Sioux in the net.

Major Reno, who ended up without a command of his own, prepared for the next day's march then spent the rest of the evening drinking heavily.

Later, Lieutenant Winfield Edgerly walked up to the regimental headquarters and visited with Lieutenant Cooke.

> I went to the Regimental Headquarters and sat down with Col. Cook [Lieutenant William Cooke]....
>
> Soon the General [Custer] came out of his tent and I said "General, won't we step high if we do get those fellows!" He replied, "Won't we!" adding, "It all depends on you young officers. We can't get Indians without hard riding and plenty of it!"[7]

Meanwhile, Willie Cooke was feeling some pangs of apprehension about the upcoming battle. He went to Lieutenant Gibson's tent, asking his fellow officer to witness his will.

Gibson laughed. "What, getting cold feet, Cookie, after all these years with the savages?"

"No," said Cooke, "but I have a feeling that the next fight will be my last."

Jack Sturgis fell on Gibson's cot laughing. "Oh, listen to the old woman. Bet he's been to see a fortune teller," he said.[8]

Newspaper reporter Mark Kellogg spent the evening writing his article for the *New York Herald*. He enclosed a private note indicating to the editor that the officers of the Seventh had written to their friends to watch for his reports in the *Herald* "as they know I am going to record their deeds."

His newspaper article gave a vivid view of the western countryside to the eastern readership, and extravagantly extolled the merits of the Seventh Cavalry in general and Lieutenant-Colonel Custer and General Terry in particular. He described the past week's march up the valley of the Yellowstone which impressed him as a river. "Its color resembles yellowish clay at this point. It is cool and pleasant to the taste ... the waters of the Tongue River are of a deepish red color, running swiftly, and not very palatable to the taste."

Kellogg envisioned the white man's move into the west, describing the valley "of the magnitude and facilities it affords for commercial purposes in the near future, when its beautiful valley shall become populated...."

He noted that they had passed by a large camp, long-abandoned, which would have contained 1,500 Indian lodges, and expressed the prevalent lust for killing the Indians. "The hope is now strong and I believe, well founded, that this band of ugly customers, known as Sitting Bull's band, will be 'gobbled' and dealt with as they deserve."

Kellogg ended the article by extolling the virtues of General Terry whom he described as "large brained, sagacious, far reaching, cool under all circumstances and with rare executive abilities."

And his obviously star-struck assessment of Custer called him

> the most peculiar genius in the army, ... possessing electrical mental capacity and of iron frame and constitution; ... who has warm friends and bitter enemies; ... a man to do right as he construes the

right, in every case; one respected and beloved by
his followers who would freely follow him into the
"jaws of hell."[9]

He attached a note to all of this for his editor, Lounsberry, at the
Bismarck Tribune: "We leave the Rosebud [Creek] tomorrow, and by
the time this reaches you we will have met and fought the red devils,
with what results remains to be seen. I go with Custer...."[10]

When his writing was done, Kellogg packed pencils, a pad of
coarse gray paper, sugar, coffee, and bacon in his saddle bags. His
diary he stored in an oilcloth satchel on the mule pack train. He chose
his favourite weapon, a Spencer carbine, to take along. He was ready
for his role — reporting the battle.

Custer returned to his tent and began a letter to his wife, Libbie — a
letter he didn't finish. After assuring her of his safety, he included
General Terry's orders, orders that seemed ambiguous. Although
they gave him more leeway than the strict orders given to Major
Reno on his reconnaissance, they also set down some precise
instructions.

> I send you an extract from Genl. Terry's official
> order, knowing how keenly you appreciate words
> of commendation and confidence in your Bo: "It
> is of course impossible to give you definite instruc-
> tions in regard to this movement, and were it not
> impossible to do so, the Department Commander
> places too much confidence in your zeal, energy,
> and ability to impose on you precise orders which
> might hamper your action when nearly in contact
> with the enemy."[11]

Custer didn't finish his letter. The orders from General Terry continued in part: "He [General Terry] will however indicate to you his own views of what your action should be, and he desires that you should conform to them unless you see sufficient reason for departing from them...."[12] This is followed by lengthy instructions on what trail to follow and how to report to Colonel Gibbon.

Custer, with the Seventh was to go south up the Rosebud, get close to the mountains, then head west, turning north and coming down the valley of the Little Big Horn. He would march on the village; force the Sioux and Cheyenne north where their path would be blocked by Terry and Gibbon. The three commands would all meet again on June 26, after the battle. That was the plan.

Custer took no major artillery. No Gatling gun, no Napoleon gun, no sabres. He wanted nothing to slow him down. His plan was simply being first and getting the glory. And so the next morning, June 22, the Seventh Cavalry passed in review before General Terry and Colonel Gibbon. Custer had a reputation of surging ahead, looking for glory, and there was a sense he would do so again.

CHAPTER 23

HEADING TO LITTLE BIGHORN

T HE SEVENTH REGIMENT MADE ITS WAY UP THE ROSEBUD
Valley on a typical June day, crabapple trees and wild roses in
bloom. They saw signs of Indian activity, including a relatively fresh
scalp on a stick. Then a more ominous sign — a circular arbour about
200 feet in circumference, and in the middle a pile of buffalo heads,
signifying the site of a Sun Dance. This was an annual Plains Indian
ritual that, with the Lakota, sometimes involved self-torture, such as
Sitting Bull took part in. Some government and army officials feared
it, because to them it signified a bringing together of the Indians,
strengthening their numbers.

Farther up Rosebud Creek the Indian trail was nearly a mile
wide, the earth dug up by travois poles, resembling a ploughed field.
The regiment set up camp for a rest. Custer decided he wanted to get
closer to the ridge before daylight, so they resumed their march at
11:00 that night.

Before 3:00 a.m. the advance scouts were on a knoll, able to see
into the valley of the Little Bighorn. They spotted the Indian village
below. A message was sent back to where Custer and the regiment
were having breakfast in camp, about twelve miles east. Smoke from
the Seventh's camp fires could be seen twelve miles away on the knoll.

Custer, still unaware that Crook was nowhere around, decided
that before attacking he would send Major Marcus Reno to the
immediate south.

The Seventh had about 675 men, including the Indian scouts,
guides, and fifteen of the seventeen Canadians. George Hayward

of Company I was sick in the camp hospital at Fort Lincoln when Custer's expedition had left in May. George Anderson was on detached service at the time and didn't accompany the regiment. The Crow scouts wore red arm bands to help the soldiers identify them from the Indians they would be fighting. The Crows called Custer "Son of the Morning Star," while for the Arikaras he was "Long Hair."

Though the Indians were well armed with repeating rifles from traders, the cavalry regiment counted on the army issue regulation single-shot, breech loading 1873 Springfield carbines. This weapon had greater range, but its cartridges would occasionally heat up and jam when fired, and had to be pried loose. But it was a cheaper gun. The enlisted men also carried side-arm pistols. Each man had 100 rounds of carbine ammunition and twenty-four pistol cartridges. The pack mules carried 26,000 additional carbine rounds. Some officers and a few sergeants supplied their own, more expensive arms. Custer carried a Remington sporting rifle, hunting knife in a beaded scabbard, and two stubby English revolvers on his belt.[1]

The troopers marched away from the Rosebud and by late afternoon Custer called a halt. After setting up camp and finishing the evening meal, Custer called his officers for a briefing. With officers squatting around the small tent shelter, he talked about his expectations. He expected to meet up to 1,500 or more Indians, a different story than he had told them earlier on. He said he intended to stay the course until they found the Indians, even if it was much longer than General Terry had intended.

Custer did not tell his subordinates of the grand strategy devised by Terry. His officers, much less the enlisted men, knew little or nothing of the plan to meet the Montana Column somewhere near the mouth of the Little Bighorn on the 26th.[2]

[Lieutenant Edward] Godfrey returned to his bivouac with Lts. McIntosh and [George] Wallace, and as they walked together Wallace said, "I believe

General Custer is going to be killed." Godfrey
asked why he thought so. Wallace answered that
he had never heard the general talk like that [be so
conciliatory].[3]

On June 24, while coming across a deserted Indian camp site,
they found a white man's scalp and other signs the scouts inter-
preted as meaning the Sioux knew the enemy was coming and meant
to win the battle. Sergeant Vickory stuck the staff of his flag in the
ground. When it fell down and pointed to the rear, the superstitious
Lieutenant Wallace said it boded ill for Custer.

By about 5:00 p.m. they resumed the march, following a trail
that had some camp fires still smouldering, the valley scarred from
thousands of trailing lodge poles dragged along by the Indians.

More than two hours later, the Seventh stopped to rest. The trail
turned west and crossed toward the valley of the Little Bighorn. The
Indians were nearby. Terry's orders had said if the trail turned away
from Rosebud Creek, Custer was to make a loop, go south to the
headwaters of the Tongue before turning west to the Little Bighorn.
He would then follow the river northward. Custer disobeyed those
orders. He felt the Seventh was too close to the Indian camp and
had already been spotted. Custer and the Seventh would follow
their trail.[4]

The scouts out front had returned with news of a summit
between the Rosebud and the Little Bighorn, and a hollow where
they could hide both men and horses. The regiment moved out just
after 11:00 that night, June 24. Custer's plan was to take a day to
reconnoitre the village and attack on the early morning of the 26th.

It was a rough trail through the dark of night. The mule train fell
behind. When ammunition packs came loose, the troopers cut them
off and left them as they had been ordered to do. Losing ammunition.
By two in the morning, Custer called a halt to rest, having made eight
miles of the twelve-mile distance to the cliff edge.

The message back from the scouts this time told of seeing the village from the summit. Custer issued the order to be ready to go at 8:00 a.m. By this time the forward scouting group was sure they had been spotted by Indians from the village. The Crows finally convinced Custer they'd been spotted and they shouldn't wait for the next day to attack. There were other signs that they had been spotted; when a soldier from Company F, Myers' company, backtracked to pick up supplies that had been accidentally dropped along the way, he spotted Indians on their trail.

Custer reached the knoll mid-morning on Sunday, June 25. There had not been any great effort to be quiet on the advance — mules braying, troopers hallooing, and frying pans banging. Custer surveyed from the knoll using a telescope and binoculars, but apparently couldn't see clearly what was below. And despite being warned that it was the largest Indian gathering ever seen by his officers, Custer decided to attack. He seemed assured the Sioux were locked in — Crook to the south, the Sioux enemies, the Crow, to the west, Terry and Gibbon at the north.

A much-needed day of rest was abandoned. More men, about 130 troopers, were assigned to protect the ammunition pack train. Custer abandoned plans to send a message to Terry. The Indian village was near. The Seventh would strike immediately. Custer's concern was not the size of the village; he didn't want to allow the Indians to scatter and get away.

CHAPTER 24

CUSTER SPLITS HIS COMMAND

C USTER HAD BEEN RIDING HIS OLD HORSE DANDY AND WANTED a fresh one for the battle. He had his striker saddle up his fresh mount Victory. He led the command out in columns of four, each company separated. Lieutenant Cooke rode by his side. Sergeant Vickory, with the guidon, followed close by. Then came the Italian trumpeter, Martini.

A few minutes after noon on June 25, almost a mile farther on, Custer called a halt to make battalion assignments. He and Cooke rode off a ways to talk, the adjutant scribbling in his notebook, probably assessing the strengths of various divisions.[1]

In what was later considered a controversial move, Custer split his troops into four parts, in the process cutting the left wing in half.

Captain Frederick Benteen took three companies of the left wing, Companies D, H, and K, to search the badlands to the left. Richard Saunders and James Harris were in that battalion. The subaltern was Katie Garrett Gibson's husband, Lieutenant Frank Gibson.

Major Marcus Reno was assigned the remaining three companies of the left wing, A, G, and M, to head down the valley, cross the Little Bighorn River, and attack. Donald McIntosh commanded Company G, James Weeks rode with the Company M troops. This assignment was considered a blow by Reno since he didn't have a full wing of six companies under his command.

Custer would follow Reno with the right wing, minus Captain Thomas McDougall's Company B, which would stay behind with the mule pack train. Three Canadians went with McDougall. Charles

Orr, originally signed up with Company C, and John McShane of Company I, were now detailed to the pack train. Thomas Seayers was sent from Company A to the pack train as well.

Custer's five companies were C, E, F, I, and L. The Canadians along with Custer were Frank Myers and John Vickory in Company F, John McShane and Darwin Symms in Company I, and Edmond Tessier and Andrew Snow in Company L. Regimental Adjutant Lieutenant William "Willie" Cooke rode with Custer out front. Kellogg, atop a mule, managed to get a spot with the Custer group.

MacAdams, the seventeenth Canadian, was in the Second Cavalry, which was with Colonel Gibbon's Montana Column.

Sergeant Vickory had been named standard bearer. He carried Custer's personal headquarters flag — a swallow-tailed guidon of red and blue with crossed swords, the same as Custer had had in the Civil War. Vickory rode up front, close to Custer, as a one-flag colour party.

The Italian trumpeter, Giovanni Martini, also known as John Martin and who had once been a drummer boy for Garibaldi, had been detailed from Benteen's Company H to act as Custer's orderly.[2]

Custer had expected to hear from Benteen, but by two in the afternoon, two hours after Benteen's battalion had turned off the trail, there was still no sign of him. Meanwhile, the scouts ahead of Custer's troops reported seeing about fifty Indians riding away from an abandoned campsite.

Custer told Cooke to order Major Reno and his battalion to chase the escaping Indians. "Cooke relayed Custer's orders: 'The Indians are about two and a half miles ahead — they are on the jump. Go forward as fast as you think proper and charge them wherever you find them and he will support you.'"[3]

Reno then left with his command and moved down Rosebud Creek. He had no clear idea where Benteen had taken his troops. Almost all the scouts, Willie Cooke, and Captain Myles Keogh also rode along with Reno. The tall Canadian was one of Custer's closest friends in the regiment, and he would depend on Cooke coming back with a clear idea of what was ahead.

By 3:00 p.m. Reno's troops had followed the creek to the Little Bighorn and could see the Indians far down the valley on the other side of the river. The Little Bighorn River was about five feet deep and thirty to fifty feet wide at that point. The valley stretched along a mile of grasslands, but rugged cliffs about 300 feet high rose on the east side, creating deep ravines. A ford on the river provided access to the village.

Reno's troopers quickly crossed at the ford. Cooke and Keogh stopped there. As Company M troopers rode past, Cooke called out, "For God's sake, men, don't run those horses like that; you will need them in a few minutes."[4]

The two officers then rode back to join Custer.

Meanwhile, Reno was fortifying himself with whisky from a flask. When he was told the Indians were actually coming up the valley to meet the troops, and not running the other way as he had expected, Reno ordered his command forward. Frederic Gerard, who had been acting as a translator with the scouts, re-crossed the Little Bighorn River and headed back up the creek to warn Custer.

Reno led his command down the valley toward the fifty or so Indians he had been told to engage. He had spread two of his companies, M and A, across the valley, twenty men wide; Weeks was in Captain Keogh's Company M. Lieutenant McIntosh brought up the rear with Company G in reserve. They increased their speed down the valley. They could see the fifty Indians ahead in the dust, and beyond that a larger cloud of dust. As Major Reno, riding just behind Company A, called "Forward," at least one trooper noticed the major's voice slurred and saw him lift the whisky flask once again.

Custer was left with a fragmented command of about 220 troops. Many of the officers were friends and most had adopted the buckskin jacket that Custer wore. Some had stripped down to their wide collared blue shirts in the afternoon Montana heat.

Within twenty minutes Cooke, Keogh, and Gerard had all returned with the news. The Indians were not retreating but getting ready to meet the attack.

CHAPTER 25

THE ATTACK
ON THE INDIAN VILLAGE

C USTER'S CONTINGENT PAUSED ON A RIDGE WHILE THE officers surveyed the village in the distance through their field glasses. Before them was the largest gathering of Indians they had ever seen. The tribes were camped in six circles. At the north was the Cheyenne circle. Leading south along the west bank of the river were the circles of the Sans Arcs, Miniconjoux, Oglalas, Blackfeet, and Sitting Bull's Unkpapas or Hunkpapas.

Sitting Bull had sent word earlier in the spring to agency Indians, those on reservations, to join him. Hundreds did. Following game they had moved north into the valley of Greasy Grass River, what white people called the Little Bighorn. They included both Cheyenne and Sioux. Custer's Indian scouts could probably identify who were in the village from the appearance of the lodges. Sioux lodges or teepees were tall and narrow with a big flap opening at the top. Cheyenne lodges were shorter, more squat, with small flaps for ventilation.

The warriors were stirring up the dust to allow the women and children to escape. These warriors had been up all night celebrating the victory over Crook. Some of the young warriors had been doing a "Dying Dance," anticipating a battle with the soldiers to avenge their friends and family killed in the recent Rosebud River battle with Crook.

From the ridge Custer's troops could see Reno's command heading down the valley, toward the huge village, unsuspecting of what it would meet. Custer told Cooke they needed Benteen's troops. The adjutant passed this along to Captain Tom Custer of Company C who ordered one of his men to go back to McDougall, tell him to hurry up the pack train. The message was that if he saw Benteen he should tell him to come quickly since there was a big Indian camp up ahead.

Some of the scouts went ahead of Reno down the valley. They weren't intended to fight, but for the Arikaras this was an opportunity to get back at their enemy, the Sioux. Their job was to gather as many horses as they could for the troops. But some of them decided to fight their enemy the Sioux instead.

Meanwhile Donald "Tosh" McIntosh took part in the opening charge on the southern end of the village. Reno ordered Lieutenant McIntosh and Company G up to his right flank. Now he was moving down the valley with his three companies stretched right across. Up ahead they could see the fifty Indians they had been chasing. The Indians were moving back and forth raising a cloud of dust. Reno and his troops couldn't see behind that huge cloud; couldn't see the huge village with its warriors. He had sighted Custer riding down the valley across the river, but Reno had not received any new orders by courier. He had been told to chase the fifty Indians down the valley and he had no plan to follow up with a larger engagement. Reno ordered his battalion to halt, dismount and fight on foot. His adjutant Lieutenant Benny Hodgson relayed the order to McIntosh's Company G on the right.

A few troopers with horses continued right into the cloud of dust with the Indians, others were designated horse-holders and took the mounts into the woods. This left about 100 troopers standing or lying on the battlefield, shooting at the warriors in the swirling dust. The time was about 3:30 p.m. on June 25.

Before long the battalion began to move into the woods. McIntosh took his Company G into the wooded area and Major Reno went as well. Meanwhile, Company A moved over to fill the gap in the line.

Custer could see Reno's battalion in its fight. He and Lieutenant Cooke waved their hats at Reno as they saw his troopers move into the woods. Custer dismissed his Crow scouts and led his command eastward down a narrow ravine.

For the Cheyenne it was a time for revenge — time to avenge both Black Kettle's massacre eight years previous, and the Sand Creek Massacre. Many warriors still sleeping off the long night of dancing rushed from the lodges looking for their horses, some stopping to don battle paint or dress.

> Sitting Bull helped his nephew [One Bull] prepare for battle, giving him a stone-headed war club and his own rawhide shield; then he buckled on his cartridge belt and went outside. He mounted a black horse and rode off to encourage those gathering to counterattack. While One Bull and other warriors charged the far end of the soldiers' line, Sitting Bull, White Bull [another nephew], and other Lakotas moved forward to a shallow draw that ran across the valley just south of the camp. From there they traded furious fire with the bluecoats, who had dismounted and planted three guidons out on the prairie.[1]

It wasn't long before hundreds of Indians began to outflank Reno's troops, about 500 or more riding around his left flank. Reno ordered the men back to the woods and to get their horses. The troopers retreated to the edge of the woods, firing into the Indians galloping toward them. The air was thick with dust, the roar of guns, and the shrieks of the Indian warriors.

Donald McIntosh led his men to charge a part of the village down through the woods, Reno still with him. Meanwhile, Company A was running out of ammunition on the line. The horses were brought up so the troops could get at their saddlebags and the extra ammunition.

Just then the fiercest of all, Oglala war chief Crazy Horse, joined the battle. He had taken time to apply his paint and ready himself. As he made his way toward the fighting mounted on his pinto pony, hundreds more warriors joined him, surrounding the woods where Reno had his troops.

> The Indians waited till enough of them got together. Crazy Horse said to his followers: "Here are some of the soldiers after us again. Do your best, and let us kill them all today, that they may not trouble us anymore. All ready! Charge! Himself leading the assault.... The Indians chased the soldiers across the river, killing about 40. They chased them up on the bluff or high point where the [pack] train was, and had the soldiers corralled in a small place.[2]

For Reno, there was no sign of Custer or Benteen. Earlier he had seen Custer and Cooke wave their hats from the cliff top but had not seen them since. Reno believed his position was untenable, and decided to retreat and head for the high cliffs to regroup with the rest of the regiment. But what followed was total confusion. The order given by the major could not be heard above the thunder of the Indian warfare, and Company G didn't have a trumpeter to sound the call.

As Reno tried to direct the men to retreat, a round of fire hit Bloody Knife, Custer's favourite scout, his blood spraying the major in the face. This led to panic on the major's part. Many of the men were still on foot when Reno yelled, "Any of you men who wish to make your escape, draw your revolvers and follow me." Reno spurred his horse out of the woods, down the dry riverbed a short way, and up onto the prairie.[3]

Company A straggled up out of the woods behind Reno, with Company M troops right behind. Some of Company G followed.

Donald McIntosh had been trying to gather his scattered troops when the order came to leave the woods so was late in joining the retreat.

He was unable to locate his orderly, Private John Rapp, and his personal mount "Shakespeare." Private Samuel McCormick of Company G, offered him his own mount, saying he was going to remain in the woods and take his chances. [It was his horse Puff.] McIntosh accepted his offer, and rode through the woods to the dry riverbed, where he encountered Private Thomas O'Neil, Company G, and asked him where the command was? O'Neil told him the command had left.... McIntosh spurred from the riverbed onto the open plain.[4]

The confused chaotic retreat, with its mad roar of sound and swirling of dust, could not have been what McIntosh envisioned when he said goodbye to Molly at Fort Abraham Lincoln those weeks ago. First his horse was killed by an arrow to the head. He jumped onto another horse but was unable to get away. His desperate ride to catch up to the battalion was witnessed by several troopers, including Private Roman Rutten of Company M.

He was singled out by himself, and was trying to urge his horse along, but was not succeeding well. His lariat was dragging, which seemed to bother the horse. McIntosh was surrounded by twenty or thirty Indians who were circling him, apparently determined to get him.[5]

Private Theodore R. Goldin, Company G, said he witnessed McIntosh's fall:

I saw McIntosh when he went down and only noticed that he did not regain his feet. I was perhaps fifty yards to the left and a bit to the rear when I saw his horse go down.... I noticed that his lariat was dragging on the ground, once in a while catching in the tall grass or sage bush and then breaking loose and the picket pin bounding into the air....[6]

Donald McIntosh, part Chippawa Indian, who had left the land of his mother's people in Canada, died at the hands of the Plains Indians who were fighting what they saw as a last battle to keep the land of their birth.

Major Reno led his ragged column out of the woods and the Indians soon realized they were not being attacked, but that the soldiers were travelling across the valley. At this the warriors stayed their distance but rode abreast of them, shooting sideways into the troops, dealing death blows. A very few troopers stayed behind in the woods, knowing the Indians' reluctance to be drawn into the forest for a fight.

Gall and his warriors had turned Reno's flank and forced him into the woods. He then frightened Reno into making a hasty retreat, which the Indians quickly turned into a rout. "The result made it possible for Gall to divert hundreds of warriors for a frontal attack against Custer's column, while Crazy Horse and Two Moon struck the flank and rear."[7]

Troopers were dying in groups of ten or fifteen as they broke away from the column. When Reno finally reached the river it was at a spot forty feet wide and about four feet deep. The banks were high on both sides. There was a small trail leading to a ford, which soon became clogged with men and horses. The stream soon flowed red as the warriors, shooting from the riverbank, picked off the troopers, shooting from the river bank.

All this time Reno had not ordered any cover for the men at the rear, and in fact he scrambled ahead, across the river, and up a ravine leading to the bluffs. There were warriors on some of the bluffs picking off the troopers as they made their way forward. Reno still called it not a retreat but a charge.

> About half of Reno's shattered column had made it to the bluffs unscathed. Twenty-nine enlisted men and three officers lay dead in the valley below, where at that moment, all along Reno's route to the river, Indians in plain view were ransacking their bodies for clothing, ammunition, and other possessions, scalps included. Nearly twenty others were missing, quite possibly still in the timber, maybe dead.[8]

The Canadian Private James Weeks, with Captain Thomas French's Company M, was able to get out of the battlefield with others during the attack on the southern end of the village. They fled across the Little Bighorn River ford to the safety of the bluffs where Custer had last been seen. The young Nova Scotian dug a trench in the sand with his knife and tin cup and settled in for the fight. There the troopers were pinned down by Indian sharpshooters.

The injured were suffering from their wounds, the heat of the sun, and lack of water. Jim Weeks volunteered. From the cliff top he made his way down a ravine, ran the last few yards in the open to get water from the river. At the water's edge he dipped his head in the river and drank, then filled a kettle and ran back to the ravine. He struggled to the top with his bounty. "Upon returning, Jim was called to by Captain Miles [sic] Moylan. 'Give me a drink!' shouted Captain Moylan. 'You go to hell and get your own water, this is for the wounded,' replied Weeks."[9]

Many of the Indian women and children were escaping north into the hills, but Pretty White Buffalo decided escape was not for her. She wanted to watch the warriors overthrow the soldiers. She could only do that from nearer to the fight that would begin when the soldiers approached the river at the lower end of the village. "I knew," she said, "that no man who rode with Long Hair would go back to tell the tale."

> The camp was not pitched for a fight and no one had anticipated any. The men would not have set up the camp in such a way as to invite attack from both ends and from the middle. No, thought Pretty White Buffalo, what was happening that day was done while the sun stood still. The Great Spirit had delivered the white men into the hands of the Lakota.[10]

Gall wanted to ensure that his family was safe since there had already been some shooting right into the village. It was after 4:30 p.m. He had seen some Arikaras shooting at his people. Gall made his way to the nearly deserted Hunkpapa camp.

> His lodge was vacant. He extended his search around the point of timber a short distance to the south. There he finally found his family. Dead. His two wives and his three children, killed. The *wasichus* [white people] or their Ree allies did get in close enough to the camp to wage their war on the defenseless ones. Gall was crushed. For all his strength and fortitude, he had not been there to protect them....
> "It made my heart bad," he said. "After that I killed all my enemies with the hatchet." Gall finally mounted back up and rode for the river crossing.[11]

Meanwhile, from his point on the ridge, Custer decided to go down, cross the river, and capture the village. Then, he reasoned, the warriors would have to surrender rather than endanger the village with a shootout.

CHAPTER 26

THE BATTLE OF LITTLE BIGHORN

A T A NARROW RAVINE CUSTER PAUSED HIS COMMAND AND decided to send an order to Benteen to join the main column and bring the extra ammunition packs. He once again turned to his adjutant, Cooke. The courier would be Giovanni Martini or John Martin as he was known. Not trusting Martin's limited command of the English language, Cooke tore a page from his pocket notebook and wrote the order. This final message from Custer's command read:

> Benteen. Come on. Big Village.
> Be quick. Bring Packs.
> P.S. Bring Packs.
> W.W. Cooke[1]

Martin turned and rode back up the ravine. At his last sight of the Custer command, they were galloping down the river heading north in the direction of the Indian village.

Custer devised a plan. It called for the taking of hostages as he did at Washita — the women and children. He decided to split his company once again, sending two companies of the troops to a second ford in the river to pretend a crossing, thereby diverting the warriors from Reno's troops, giving them some relief. Captain Keogh of Company I would head the three companies which would accompany Custer further north. By this time, Benteen would join them with his three companies. Custer would then have six companies, which would join with the two diversion companies, and together all eight companies would storm the village.

Captain George Yates of Company F would take two companies to the second ford to create the diversion. This included the Quebec farmer Frank Myers. Sergeant Vickory, also of Company F, stayed with Custer as the flag bearer.

Darwin Symms of Montreal and George Hayward of Walton, Ontario, were both in Company I, but Hayward was sick in hospital back at Fort Lincoln. Symms stayed with Captain Keogh and Custer. They would ride the ridge above the river as it twisted to the north. Rifle fire in a volley would signal Yates to join them.

Captain Frederick Benteen had ridden to the southwest with three companies as originally instructed, the Canadians Saunders and Harris among the troopers. They moved across the hills, looking down into valley after valley, searching for the elusive Indians. Captain Benteen sent Lieutenant Frank Gibson on ahead with an escort to get to the highest lookouts and direct the column. Hill after hill, valley after valley, showed no sign of the Natives. After approximately two hours, Benteen made an abrupt turn, and led his column north, back to Custer's original trail. For some reason, he didn't send a courier with a message to let Custer know about this change.

Benteen made no effort to hurry back. In fact, the mule train nearly caught up to them when they stopped to water horses. As they moved further up the trail they could hear gunfire and met the first courier taking a message to the pack train to hurry up.

A mile or so after that, they met Private Martin galloping toward them. Martin carried the message pencilled by Cooke. When questioned by Benteen, Martin, in his heavily accented English, said that Major Reno was charging the camp and killing men, women, and children right and left[2] — a story that was far from the truth.

Benteen was confused about the order from Custer. How could he bring up the mule train, but hurry toward Custer at the same time? He sent Martin with an order for the mule train to hurry, and he set his column forward at a faster pace. When they reached the point in the trail where Custer had split his command, Benteen sent Captain Thomas Weir and Company D left toward the river; this included the Nova Scotian Richard Saunders. Lieutenant Godfrey and Company K took the hill trail. The Canadian Anderson of Company K was on detached service back at Fort Lincoln. Benteen and Gibson's Company H rode between. As the gunfire sounded closer, the troopers formed a line and broke into a gallop.

The Sioux had set the valley grasses on fire and this, combined with the clouds of dust, made it difficult for Benteen to determine what was happening. After meeting some Crow scouts, they were directed to Reno's ragged column on the bluff.

As they approached, a much-excited Major Reno, red handkerchief tied around his head, rode out to meet them. "For God's sake, Benteen, halt your command and help me," he shouted. "I've lost half my men." He told Benteen what had happened. "We are whipped," he said.[3]

Though Benteen showed the major the note urging them to hurry to Custer and the village, Reno insisted they wait for the pack train since his men were short on ammunition as well. Weir, having met up with them on the bluffs, ordered his Company D in a line. And Godfrey with Company K formed a line along the bluffs.

The warriors harassing Reno's troops withdrew and rode north downstream. Meanwhile, the troopers could see the warriors scalping and mutilating the bodies of their fallen comrades in the valley below. It was brought to Reno's attention by a member of Benteen's column, but Reno made no effort to order a rescue detail.

They seemed to have no idea where Custer was. They finally began hearing gunfire downstream. But Reno's command remained where it was as the roar of battle increased.

Foolish Elk had crossed the river at the broad ford
with Crazy Horse but saw other Indians crossing

farther downstream. There were so many he wondered how such a small force of soldiers would stand a chance against them....

While Custer followed the line of ridges, the Indians were staying abreast of him by following the hollows and ravines.... Now the battle became furious.[4]

The night before, during the "dying dance," about twenty warriors, including Lakotas and several Cheyennes, had taken a suicide vow to fight to the death in the next battle. Among those Cheyennes were Roman Nose and his son. Early the next morning they paraded through the camp. Then all went to their teepees or sweat lodges, where they stayed until the soldiers struck.[5]

The Indians rode into the hills up and down the coulees, attacking the soldiers. Sitting Bull urged them on then rode to the western side of the valley to join the older men to protect the women and children.

While the gunfire continued, Major Reno held everyone on the hill. Then he decided to go back down into the valley plain to look for his close friend, Lieutenant Benjamin Hodgson. He took the regimental doctor and a dozen troopers. They found Hodgson's body. Reno recovered Hodgson's class ring and other items but, coming under fire, they left the body where it was. He then sent one of his men to hurry up the pack train. Many officers and troopers in Benteen's command continued to question whether or not they should move up to Custer's side.

After Yates left for the river ford, Custer decided he couldn't wait any longer for Benteen. He could see Indians attacking the Yates group and ordered the signal, firing for Yates to move to the rendezvous point; Custer moved along the hills. When Yates joined them he reported some deaths, including Jack Sturgis, the son of the regiment's commanding officer.

They could see hundreds of Indians on every side. Custer decided to leave Keogh and his three companies on the high points and take Yates's smaller wing, ride along the ridge then west into the river to find the women and children to hold as hostages. He took Yates's Company F, his brother Tom's Company C, his young brother Boston, his nephew Autie, and newspaperman Mark Kellogg on his mule, heading northwest along the ridge. All in all it was about eighty men. The Canadians, William Cooke and John Vickory, accompanied Custer. Frank Myers of Company F had been transferred to the mule train.

When they neared the river they could see thousands of Indians, women and children, heading out of the village. But when they reached the river they were surprised by the number of warriors hiding in brush on the west side. Custer headed his troops back up to the ridge.

This was where Mark Kellogg disappeared in the confusion of battle. When they reached the ridge, Kellogg was not with them. He was last seen down by the river, trying to keep his mule in pace with the troopers' horses heading up the sharp incline. He was never seen alive again.

Captain Myles Keogh had Companies C, I, and L. He directed Company L along a ridge, including Canadians Edmond Tessier and Andrew Snow. Just behind, he had Company C. He held his own Company I in reserve, now with only one Canadian, Symms; McShane was back with the pack train, Hayward sick in camp at Fort Lincoln. The fighting became fiercer as Indians surrounded the position, hiding in bushes and rocks close to the soldiers.

Keogh sent a contingent down to clear the ravines leading up from the river. It was not long before arrows and gun shots from the Indians overtook the soldiers, and Lieutenant James Calhoun's Company L was overrun with Indians firing repeaters. Tessier and Snow went down in that onslaught.

Oglala Sioux's Crazy Horse led a band of warriors across the river. They dismounted and crawled up the ravine. From there they shot their arrows up into the air, coming down on the troopers.

Hunkpapa Crow King led about eighty warriors, raining an endless stream of arrows on the soldiers. Now the Indians were coming from the east, west, and south, overwhelming the soldiers, shooting and clubbing them. The air was filled with the roar of guns, screams of warriors and soldiers, and the sound of rifle and pistol fire.

Captain Keogh realized he had to get the men of Companies C and L and his own Company I to join Custer on the far end of the ridge. He jumped up onto his horse Comanche and was immediately struck by a bullet in his knee. "The round went clear through his leg into Comanche's body. Both went down."[6] Troopers from Company I gathered around their leader; the Indian warriors swarmed over them. Symms died in that battle.

Up on the ridge both Crazy Horse and White Bull had worked their way around the east side of the ridge coming in behind the soldiers. Crazy Horse challenged White Bull to a "bravery run" to cut off a large group of about sixty bluecoats.

White Bull cried, "Only heaven and earth last long!" and the two warriors whipped their horses forward, across the hills and up the east side of the ridge through a gap between the soldier groups. They leaned down over the necks of their ponies, and bullets whizzed by them as they crested the grassy ridge and rode over it, then turned and galloped back.[7]

They did this manoeuvre again and again, with others joining them. Some of the troopers threw down their rifles and used their pistols. The Indians charged through with clubs and tomahawks. Hundreds of warriors overwhelmed the troopers and killed them all. One soldier got away, around the big body of Indians, toward the north. He had a very fast horse, and the Indians were about to give up the chase when he shot himself with his revolver.[8]

CHAPTER 27

CUSTER'S LAST STAND

FOR CUSTER, IT DIDN'T LOOK GOOD. AS THE BATTLE TOOK shape Custer could see only a cloud of dust. He couldn't see Keogh's battalion, Benteen was nowhere in sight, and the Indians were slowly surrounding his position on all sides. More were running up the ridges.

Custer ordered Company E down toward them. He took the regimental staff and Company F to high ground at the edge of the ridge. Luckily for Canadian Frank Myers he was no longer in Company F, but with the pack train. Meanwhile, Richard Saunders (sometimes listed as Sanders) had been transferred from Company D to F and was with Custer's command. They shot their horses in a semi circle, facing the attackers south and south west. This formed a barricade or wall the troopers could hide behind to shoot from. A cavalry depends on its horses, so this was definitely a desperate move.

Around him Custer had his brothers, nephew, and regimental staff, including the Canadians, Lieutenant Cooke and Sergeant Vickory. The guidon was planted. Now Custer and his command were sitting on an open hill surrounded by a thousand hostile Indians.

Meanwhile, Reno and his troops had been on their hill for about an hour. At about 4:30 p.m., Captain Thomas Weir of Company D and Second Lieutenant Winfield Edgerly agreed between themselves to ride north toward Custer, where the shooting had nearly stopped. They rode northeast and made for a point a mile away.

Several troopers from Keogh's company joined Custer so he now knew that Keogh's company had been overrun. The Indians remained hidden and moved from spot to spot, making a difficult target. Men screamed amid gunfire and smoke. There were too few soldiers, and the dead horses offered meager protection.

Iron Hawk was a Hunkpapa Lakota. In 1907, he gave this account of the battle:

> Thinks Sitting Bull was at one end of the attacking Indians, Crazy Horse at one end, and Iron Hawk was on the side toward the ridge and between the ridge and the river in the attack on Custer. They surrounded Custer.
>
> Says Custer's men in the beginning shot straight, but later they shot like drunken men, firing into the ground, into the air, wildly in every way.[1]

Custer went down with his men, surrounded by members of his family and his long-time friends in the Seventh Cavalry.

> Custer took a shot in his right breast that knocked him back. He dropped his rifle and drew his English bulldog pistols. Many of the men around him were dead when another bullet smashed into his right temple and killed him instantly.... Tom Custer lay motionless, but Boston and his nephew Autie ran down the hill. They got only a hundred yards before they were shot dead.... Warriors wielding clubs and revolvers fell upon them from all sides.[2]

William Winer Cooke, astride his "almost white horse," was a long way from Upper Canada, now Ontario, where Six Nations Indians under the leadership of Chief Joseph Brant lived side by side with whites at Brant, right near his home at Mount Pleasant. In the midst of summer heat, June 25, 1876, in the Montana hills far from home, the scion of the Winer-Cooke families faced hordes of Indians intent on saving their way of life. And he lost his.

Willie Cooke, Custer's adjutant, was scalped twice — the second scalp being one of his long-flowing side whiskers or Dundrearies. Years after the battle Walter Camp interviewed an Arikara named Kanauch or Hunach who was shown photos of officers. When he saw Cooke's picture he kissed it, saying this man's very breath was kindness.

> [Cheyenne warrior] Wooden Leg, who sailed around the battlefield like a grasshopper, probably scalped Lt. Cooke's face. He said he noticed a dead soldier about thirty years old with a full mustache and a long beard growing from both cheeks ... he skinned one side of the man's face and tied the hair to an arrow shaft.[3]

Cooke's right thigh had been punctured. This was how the Sioux warriors marked a dead enemy. Since it had this cut it would seem Cooke was killed by a Sioux who scalped him. Then Wooden Leg, the Cheyenne, took the unusual beard scalp.

Raw scalps were usually turned over to the women who prepared them for exhibit. Wooden Leg's mother didn't like the look of this one with the Dundreary whiskers, but finally she accepted it and took it to her hut.

Chief of the scouts, Second Lieutenant Charles Varnum, headed down the ravine to the river to bury Hodgson as Reno had ordered. Death caught up with Bennie Hodgson and Donald McIntosh before McIntosh's disciplinary charges against the second lieutenant were ever resolved.

Some members of Company G who had stayed in the woods came up the ravine with Herenden. Benteen thought the entire command was moving north with Weir, so he got ammunition that had been brought up from the pack train. He ordered H, K, and M companies after Weir. Canadian George Anderson of Company K would have been with this group, but fortunately for him he had been on detached service from his company since May 17 and was back at Fort Abraham Lincoln. Captain Thomas French led his Company M north, the only one from Reno's battalion to do so. Canadian James Weeks moved forward in Company M. There were still no orders from Major Reno.

Captain McDougall brought up Company B and the mule pack train, which included the five Canadians. When he found Reno drinking, McDougall put out a skirmish line on his own.

Varnum was called back just after he reached Hodgson's body. To the north the men could see about 1,500 warriors.

Reno ordered a halt by trumpeter but other officers ignored him. Reno finally followed McDougall's company.

It became apparent to Benteen that the new position on a ridge was untenable. Indians were coming fast and furious about 700 yards away. Major Reno agreed with Benteen to withdraw to the original position on the bluffs overlooking the Little Bighorn. McDougall asked Benteen to take over command; after that orders supposedly by Reno had actually been suggested by Benteen.

The retreat began with Lieutenant Godfrey and Second Lieutenant Edgerly doing a proper retreat procedure with Companies K and D — firing methodically, pulling each platoon back a short distance, kneeling, and firing alternately.

The position they held was a large saucer-like area bordered by low ridges, and on the west side dropping to the river a quarter mile away. In the middle surrounded by mules, a hospital was established. As the Indians fell back they occupied every bit of high ground around the soldiers.

As the afternoon stretched on, a pattern emerged.

The Indians would pour a heavy fire into the

position, their guns emitting a thick ring of smoke surrounding the regiment. Then they would work their nerve up to make a charge, at which time the troopers would pop up and fire, scattering them back to the hills. This went on until sunset and beyond.[4]

They had almost no water, no access to water, a limited supply of ammunition, and a poor defensive position with thousands of Indians surrounding them. Major Reno spent most of his time near the hospital. Later reports indicated Lieutenant Frank Gibson had spent much of the time dug in behind the mule pack train.

Down in the valley that night the Indians built fires. The drums were beaten, there was singing and dancing in celebration and wailing for their dead. Reno suggested they withdraw, leaving their wounded. This outrageous suggestion was vetoed by Captain Benteen.[5]

At dawn the next day, June 26, the rifle fire began anew and lasted throughout most of the day. At 3:00 p.m. the Indians set fire to the grass to cover their movement out of the valley. In the early evening the troopers stood up to watch the cavalcade of the village up the valley, heading south toward the Bighorn Mountains. Some estimates say there were about 7,000 people with about 20,000 horses. Indian guards stayed behind to watch until dark. Later that night, the remaining troopers of the Seventh moved closer to the river.

CHAPTER 28

GENERAL TERRY
TO THE RESCUE

THE INDIANS OF THE MID-AND-NORTHWEST WERE BEING squeezed from the plains and Black Hills by the white migration, and they knew it. They saw this battle as a victory for their land and a revenge for past wrongs by the United States government and army. They wanted to be left alone on their land to hunt, fish, and follow the buffalo as they had for centuries; mutilating the troops was an age-old custom.

> They failed to see why they should live in one place all year, why they should become farmers when they had been hunters.... They thought the earth was created for everybody, that it could not be appropriated by individuals or groups....
>
> So the squaws, weeping for a dead husband or dead brother or son, hacked at naked white corpses with butcher knives and axes, lopped off fingers, hands, penises, and battered the skulls of dying cavalrymen with stone mallets.[1]

On June 26, the day after Custer's Last Stand, the Sioux and Cheyennes dismantled their village and began to make their way to the Bighorn Mountains. By the second night they were about twenty miles south and they staged a victory dance. Sitting Bull's Hunkpapa Sioux didn't participate, thinking it too soon, a time of mourning rather than rejoicing.

In the battle, the Seventh Cavalry lost the five companies, C, E, F, I, and L, under Custer — about 210 men. Of the other companies of the regiment, under Major Reno and Captain Benteen, fifty-three men were killed and fifty-two wounded.[2]

As planned, General Terry left the Yellowstone base camp on June 24, aiming to meet up with Custer's command two days later. This included men from the Montana column under Colonel John Gibbon. So General Terry's column of 400 men included four cavalry units, five infantry troops, and an artillery unit. The Canadian, James George Macadams, was in the Second Cavalry with the Montana column. They headed north up the Little Bighorn. It was a late start. The next day, June 25, they marched on, getting lost and not making much time. By evening, General Terry asked the cavalry units to ride ahead, which they did, pulling up at midnight.

Early on the morning of June 26, a couple of Custer's Crow scouts met Terry's forward command and told of Custer's defeat, but everyone thought this was an exaggeration. As they approached the valley they saw smoke but thought it was Custer burning the Indian village. By noon, the command had crossed the Little Bighorn, moving upstream on the east side. In the distance they saw hundreds of Indians wearing U.S. Army clothing and knew something was terribly wrong.

General Terry stopped all of his units for the evening.

At dawn on June 27, two days after the day Custer had met his Waterloo, Terry's command came to the abandoned village. "When troopers came across pieces of cavalry equipment — saddles, clothes, the feet of top boots — and three severed heads of white men, they began to fear the worst."[3]

As the command continued around the bend of the river and through the village they began to find bodies, bodies of white men, mutilated and swarming with flies. And the soldiers thought one of them was Custer. They could also see men standing on the bluff on the opposite side of the river. Two of the Seventh Cavalry officers met them, telling Terry they hadn't seen Custer and his command for the past two days. General Terry broke the news that they had found him, dead.

Captain Benteen took some officers and headed north, following Custer's trail. They soon found the bodies of Lieutenant James Calhoun's Company L, which included Canadians Andrew Snow and Edmond Tessier. North of that were the bodies of Captain Keogh and Company I, including Canadian Darwin Symms. They spotted another forty troopers down the ridge, most of them from Captain George Yates' Company F, including the Canadian Richard Saunders.

> George Custer was found near the southwestern edge of the elevation, behind a horse, his right leg across the body of a soldier, while his back was lumped against the body of two others. The latter two were identified as probably being Sergeant John Vickory, the regimental color bearer, who lay with his face up. The second body was identified as that of chief trumpeter Henry Voss, who lay across Vickory's head, Voss' face being down. Vickory had his right arm cut off at the shoulder. Some 20 feet back from Custer lay the extremely mutilated body of Tom Custer.... Lt William Cooke, his thighs slashed and one of the black whiskers scalped was found between two horses close to Tom.[4]

Now the burial work began. The wounded were moved to the Montana column camp, and the rest of the day was spent in burying the bodies. The burials continued into the next day. These were summary operations; there were few shovels, the earth was dry, and many bodies were barely covered. They found and treated the only surviving horse that remained, Comanche, Captain Keogh's horse. Keogh himself was dead.

General Terry moved out the troops, heading for the steamer the *Far West*. On the way, they spotted the body of Mark Kellogg, and buried him. The wounded were put aboard the steamer, including the horse Commanche. The *Far West* made its way down the Little Bighorn to the Yellowstone River, then to Fort Abraham Lincoln — about 700 miles. It pulled in to Bismarck across from the fort on July 5. At dawn, July 6, it crossed the Missouri River to the post.

The fort surgeon Dr. Middleton, two members of his staff, the fort commander Captain McCaskell, and Lieutenant Gurley went to break the news to the wives. Elizabeth Custer went with them to tell the wives in officers' quarters and the wives of the troops.

> Captain McCluskey [the surgeon's staff member] could never forget how Mrs. Calhoun had run after him — her brothers Armstrong [George Armstrong Custer], Tom, Boston; her nephew Autie Reed, her husband Jimmie — "Is there no message for me?" she asked.
>
> Message? They had all died fighting.[5]

CHAPTER 29

BURYING THE BODIES

THERE ARE INDICATIONS CANADIAN WILLIE COOKE MAY HAVE been one of the last of the Seventh Cavalry to die that day. In reporting the news of the battle, the Chicago *Times Herald* wrote: "Dr. Cooke has been informed by the Indians that his son was the last of Custer's men to fall and apparently had been shot several times before he succumbed."

There has been some question about Lieutenant Cooke's bravery in battle. Cooke apparently did lead several charges against the Indians, which are points in his favour militarily. Against him is the fact his body was found on Last Stand Hill, not near the river.

Cooke, along with the rest of the battle casualties, was buried hastily in the field by the troops who arrived with General Terry. He was buried first by Sergeant John M. Ryan. A year later, in 1877, he was exhumed and buried at Custer Battlefield National Monument (now Little Bighorn Battlefield National Monument). Barely a month later, however, he was exhumed for a second time and moved to his final resting place in Hamilton. Friends from Brantford and Hamilton, along with Cooke's brother Dr. Cooke, travelled to Montana to exhume the body from its shallow grave. His remains were placed in a rough wooden box and taken home by train.[1]

Cooke was finally buried in Hamilton cemetery, the resting place of the city's famous pioneers and founders. On August 1, 1877, he was placed in the Winer family plot, Christ Church section. The gravestone marking the place says simply:

WILLIAM WINER
COOKE
COLONEL
7TH U.S. CAVALARY
KILLED IN ACTION
LITTLE BIG HORN
JUN 25, 1876

Norma and Ranson Cooke with the new headstone for Ranson's great-uncle,
William Winer Cooke, unveiled in Hamilton Cemetery May 28, 1983.

Courtesy of the Hamilton Spectator.

Ninety-one-year-old Myrtle Catchpole attended the ceremony to unveil the grave-stone of William Winer Cooke in Hamilton Cemetery in May, 1983. Her father was one of about 2,000 Hamilton-area veterans of the U.S. Civil War.

The "Colonel" on the headstone was the brevet rank he had managed to wring out of the U.S. Army with the help of his mother. Lieutenant Cooke shares a plot with his grandparents, John and Sarah Winer, his mother Angeline A. Cooke, and his uncle, William Dickinson Winer.

> His stone bears the crest of the Grand Army of the Republic. The original, hastily carved marker, provided by the United States government was replaced several years ago.... The original marker was given to the Monroe County Museum in the U.S. and today is on display with those which originally marked the graves of Autie [Lieutenant-Colonel George A. Custer] and Tom Custer.[2]

The new headstone was erected and dedicated by the Grand Army of the Republic on May 28, 1983. Following the deaths in the Montana hills, the Custer-Cooke family connection continued for a number of years. Cooke's parents, Dr. Alexander Hardy Cooke and his wife Angeline, had moved to Chicago. In later years, Custer's widow, Libbie, visited them often.

Late on the night of June 25, when fighting had ended, four soldiers left in the timber decided to slip away. About 10 p.m. they came upon the body of Lieutenant McIntosh "... in the hazy moonlight."

Two days later, several of the Montana Column under Colonel John Gibbon examining the Reno Battlefield observed the body of Lieutenant McIntosh. Private George C. Berry, of Gibbon's Seventh Infantry, would recall:

> A lieutenant named McIntosh was lying on his face directly in our line of march, and he had on a

buckskin shirt with his name written or printed on it. A captain of our command, who was on horseback, was riding near me when we passed this body, and said that he knew McIntosh in life and that the lieutenant was part Delaware Indian himself.[3]

McIntosh was wrestled from the saddle by the Indians and tomahawked to death. He was dragged to the riverbank and scalped from forehead to neck. General Charles F. Roe recounted the discovery of the body, naked, "the features hammed to jelly." McIntosh's brother-in-law, Lieutenant Francis Gibson of Company H, identified the badly mutilated body by an unusual Gutta-Percha button. When they found the button it was shown to Gibson as a possible way to identify the body. Gibson said, "Yes I think it will — it is my brother-in-law. Before leaving Fort Abraham Lincoln, his wife had given him these sleeve buttons."[4]

Francis Gibson was deeply shocked and saddened by the grisly mutilation of his brother-in-law. "Tosh" McIntosh, part Chippewa, showed his Indian facial features quite plainly. The Indians in battle would recognize this, consider him a traitor to his own race, and were particularly brutal in his disfigurement.

Gibson asked Private Jacob Adams of Company H to move the body by pack mule up onto Reno Hill. But Adams refused, saying he knew no way to pack it, and he buried it where it lay on the battlefield. Captain Henry B. Freeman wrote in his journal: "Lieutenants Donald McIntosh and Bennie Hodgson were found close to our camp in the valley and buried on June 27."[5]

Katie Garrett Gibson was playing the guitar with friends on the porch at Fort Rice one evening; sitting with her were the wives of Captain Benteen and of Captain Moylan. It was July, 1876. People came running across the parade ground with the news that Custer had been killed; the whole command had been killed. Not able to believe what might be rumours, the officers' wives clung together at one of the homes that night. At daybreak the steamboat brought the news. All the Fort Rice men were safe except for Jack Sturgis. For Fort Abraham Lincoln it was a different story; nearly every house was "visited by death."

From the steamboat, Katie received two letters from her husband, Lieutenant Gibson. The second one was dated after the battle at Little Bighorn. Gibson wrote to her on July 4, 1876, from a camp near the mouth of the Bighorn River: "On the twenty-seventh I buried McIntosh, and his grave is nicely marked ... poor Mollie — her heart will be completely broken...."[6]

In her grief, Mollie McIntosh recoiled from army life for some years, living with her mother. It wasn't until the birth of the Gibsons's baby girl years later that she returned to the Seventh Cavalry, now stationed at Fort Meade, Dakota. Mollie returned to Washington only when her mother became critically ill.

McIntosh's remains were interred on the battlefield on June 27, 1876. A year later, in July 1877, they were exhumed, and reburied at Arlington National Cemetery, Virginia, on August 3. In 1911, Private Roman Rutten of Company M wrote to John M Ryan: "I was talking to the man who got McIntosh's bones ready to ship to Arlington. The remains were in a cast iron box, and there was nothing but bones left. His skull was smashed in from being tommy-hawked by the squaws."[7]

Years later, Mollie Garrett McIntosh was buried beside her husband in the National Cemetery at Arlington, just at the entrance to Fort Myer.

The Canadian lieutenant had always carried a notebook or diary in his shirt pocket. This small dark notebook was found years later by Lieutenant Luther R. Hare in the possession of a Sioux woman, who had evidently picked it up near the body on the day of the battle. In the upper part was a hole caused by a bullet. His niece, Kate Gibson, remembered: "He used to carry it inside his flannel shirt. It had a bullet hole right over his heart, showing that he had been killed instantly, thank God."[8]

The diary/notebook was donated to the Little Bighorn Battlefield Museum, now the Little Bighorn Battlefield National Monument, in February, 1992. Three years later, in 1995, *The Battlefield Dispatch* gave this account of its theft and subsequent arrest of the thief:

> Rodney Adam Coronado, 28, of the Tucson Arizona area, admitted stealing First Lieutenant Donald McIntosh's diary two years ago from the Little Bighorn Battlefield Museum. Coronado said he destroyed the diary, valued at $120,000. Pleading guilty in federal court on March 3, 1995, to a count of theft of government property, he faces a maximum penalty of 10 years in prison and a fine of $250,000. Coronado gave no reason why he took the relic or why he destroyed it.
>
> The small 3 ½-inch by 6-inch diary was removed from a small Plexiglass case inside the museum.[9]

It's not clear if, in fact, the diary was actually destroyed since it probably would have been valuable on the black market. But Coronado was known as an Animal Liberation Front terrorist, so maybe he did destroy it. Coronado was released from prison in December of 2008. The diary has not been found, but the Little Bighorn Battlefield National Monument has a transcript in its records.

Mollie McIntosh was among the officers' wives who received a widow's pension from the United States government. And four years later that pension was increased. On July 2, 1890, the Senate Order showed Mrs. Mary McIntosh was included in those qualifying for more than the general monthly payment. "Other wives of second lieutenants, including Mrs. McIntosh, who, as stated, was the wife of an acting captain, have been pensioned under the general law at $17 per month. The precedent is in favor of granting the increase provided for in the bill."[10]

This was confirmed in the Committee of the Whole House on January 13, 1891. Again, it doesn't specify the amount for Mrs. McIntosh, but it indicates other captains' wives receiving $35 a month. Elizabeth C. Custer, Libbie, widow of George A. Custer, received $50 a month.

CHAPTER 30

THE FATE OF THE CANADIANS

ALTOGETHER, 263 SOLDIERS DIED ON THAT FATEFUL DAY, June 25, 1876. The Seventh Cavalry lost the five companies — C, E, F, I, and L — under Custer, a total of 210 men. Another fifty-three from the companies under Reno and Benteen were killed, and fifty-two wounded. Eight who died were Canadian, including journalist Mark Kellogg. Along with Cooke and McIntosh, there was a sergeant and four enlisted men who fell with Custer.

Sergeant John Vickory was found with his right arm severed from his body at the shoulder, his commander Lieutenant-Colonel Custer leaning on him in death. General Terry's troopers buried Vickory in the mass grave on what's now called Last Stand Hill, at the battle site. His name is listed on the Battle Monument as Jno. Vickory. In other instances, his name has also been spelled as Vickery, Victory, and Victor.

Sergeant Vickory's father, William Groesbeck, applied to the U.S. Army for his son's pension. The certificate carries the application number 286 324. The application reads "Vickory, John (alias)." It includes his service in the Second Cavalry, Union Army, during the Civil War.[1]

There were two soldiers from Yarmouth, Nova Scotia, Canada, with Custer that day — James Harris and Richard Saunders. One, James Harris, survived. The other died with his boots on.

Richard Saunders had the misfortune of being transferred from his original Company D to Company F, one of the five companies in Custer's right wing. At twenty-three years of age, not quite a year into his enlistment, Saunders died on the battlefield. He was buried in the mass grave for enlisted men. On the monument his name is written as Rich'd Saunders. He's sometimes listed as Sanders. Months later, his hometown newspaper, the *Yarmouth Herald*, carried a short notice of his death in the obituaries. "Killed in the battle of the Little Big Horn River, under Gen. Custer, June 25th, Mr. Richard Sanders, youngest son of Anthony and Aseneath Sanders, in the 22nd year of his age. Much lamented."[2]

Andrew Snow was a member of Lieutenant James Calhoun's Company L. He died on the battlefield as the whole command was overwhelmed. Snow was buried in the mass grave for enlisted men. He is listed as And'w Snow on the Battlefield Monument.

Edmond Tessier was also in Calhoun's Company L and was buried in the mass grave. He was listed as E.D. Tessier on the Battlefield Monument, as Edmund D. Tessier in the Register of Enlistments, U.S. Army, and elsewhere as Tessler.[3]

The Montrealer, Darwin L. Symms, was killed with Captain Myles Keogh's Company I. Symms was also buried in the mass grave. He is listed as D.L. Symms on the monument. His name is sometimes listed as D.L. Lymans and D.E. Symmes elsewhere.

Marcus (Mark) Henry Kellogg was the last to be buried on the battlefield. His body was found in the grass on his back, near a ravine about three quarters of a mile from Custer and 100 yards from the river. Kellogg had his clothes on; he had not been stripped as many had. Colonel John Gibbon of Montana Command said Kellogg was scalped and one ear had been cut off. The troopers in the burial party had previously overlooked Kellogg because of his isolated position. His body was spotted as General Terry took the entire contingent from the battlefield area toward the steamer the *Far West*.

The body was decomposing by the time it was found, his remains identified by one of the boots. The heel was reinforced by a piece of leather which was joined at the front with two straps. One had a buckle for tightening the boot around the foot.

Kellogg was buried June 29, 1876. It was only after 1890 that the *New York Herald* put a marker on the east slope of the battle ridge for Kellogg. Toward the end of the century, Colonel Edward G. Mathey, who by special order was in charge of the burial party, said the marker is about half a mile from the Kellogg burial spot, which is right where he fell. "I buried Mark Kellogg's body on June 29 (1876). It was the last one buried, and it lay near a ravine between Custer and the river." The body was never exhumed.[4]

Another Canadian from the east coast survived the onslaught. James Weeks returned to Fort Abraham Lincoln with the remainder of the Seventh Cavalry. But that winter, February 3, 1877, he deserted from the army. He was picked up two weeks later, but it was a short-lived return to the Cavalry. That summer, on August 26, 1877, James Weeks died of a pistol shot wound he received in a gunfight at Crow Agency, Montana. It was the result of a drunken fight at the camp on the Yellowstone River. He died within sight of the hill where he had so bravely helped his fellow soldiers the day of Custer's Last Stand by making it to the river's edge under fire and bringing back water for the wounded.[5]

Five other Canadian troopers on the expedition survived because they were fortunate enough to be transferred to the mule ammunition pack train — Harris, McShane, Myers, Orr, and Seayers.

James Harris survived the battle of Little Bighorn and stayed in the U.S. Army for another four years. It's not known if he and Saunders had been friends either before they left Yarmouth or during their time with the Seventh Cavalry. Harris was discharged on September 20, 1880, at Fort Yates, Dakota, having served out his five-year enlistment. He was considered a private of excellent character. The date and circumstances of Harris's death and burial are not known.

John McShane did well in the army after the battle at Little Bighorn. He was promoted to sergeant while at Fort Abraham Lincoln. After serving a little over two years in the Seventh, McShane was discharged on November 21, 1877, for a disability resulting from a gunshot wound. But then he met another misfortune. It is believed he was killed, possibly murdered, that winter by a man named William Costello.

Frank Myers, the young Quebec farmer, didn't last long in the army after the battle. It may have been that the horror of it haunted him. Six months after Little Bighorn, Myers deserted on December 14, 1876. He escaped capture and his date of death and place of burial are unknown.

Charles Orr stayed in the army for another four years. He was honourably discharged on September 23, 1880, at Fort Meade, Dakota, "being of good character." He was thirty-two years old. It's not known where he went from there. His date of death or place of burial is unknown.

Thomas Seayers's life in the United States cavalry played out differently. Two years almost to the day from the battle at the Little Bighorn, on June 4, 1878, Seayers deserted. He surrendered on September 28, 1878, after being three months on the loose. Seayers then faced a court martial at Fort Abraham Lincoln on February 5, 1879, as recorded in the General Court Martial Order # 4, Department of Dakota, 1879.[6]

Three other Canadians with the Seventh survived because they were elsewhere that day.

George Anderson was fortunate to be on detached service since May 17, 1876, and did not accompany his regiment into Montana for the fateful expedition. His service ended September 16 of that year, at which time he was discharged at Fort Lincoln as a "private of excellent character." Anderson never reenlisted. He died September 19, 1912, in Minneapolis and is buried there in Layman's Cemetery.[7]

George Hayward, the saddler from Walton, Upper Canada, was in hospital and didn't accompany his regiment to the Little Bighorn. He was at the fort when the news came in. Hayward stayed with the Seventh for another two years, being discharged on May 14, 1878, at the end of his service. He was considered a saddler of "excellent service." At discharge he received a pension for a disease of the lungs which may have been why he was in hospital when his fellow troopers met their fate in 1876. The date of his death and place of burial are unknown.

James George MacAdams was promoted to captain in the Second Cavalry on May 9, 1879. He seems to have settled in Montana, possibly after leaving the army, dying in Spring Creek, Montana, eleven years later on June 19, 1890, at the age of fifty-three.

The tombstones at the National Battlefield at the Little Bighorn in Montana. A man overlooks the site of Custer's Last Stand. A tall stone monument, enclosed in the fence, lists the names of the soldiers killed in battle.

Courtesy of Denver Public Library, Western Collection, x31577.

EPILOGUE

THE SEVENTEEN CANADIANS WITH LIEUTENANT-COLONEL George Armstrong Custer were men who left their home country for a job, a new life, or maybe just the adventure. Some soldiers married and adjusted to the new life — certainly Donald McIntosh did. Willie Cooke, though he never married, seemed settled in military life. Others never settled down. And, of course, some died with their boots on in the battle of Little Bighorn.

The marker for Donald McIntosh at Reno Battlefield, Montana, was put back in its original position in 1995 by Jason Pitsch, in photo. The tombstone had been moved by farmers in the 1920s. Pitsch found McIntosh's wedding ring nearby.

Courtesy of Glen Swanson.

The wedding ring of Lieutenant Donald Mcintosh, found at the Reno Battlefield by Jason Pitsch in 1995.

The body of Lieutenant William Winer Cooke was the only one to be brought back to Canada from the battlefield burial ground. Donald McIntosh and Mark Kellogg were buried individually and their graves recognized. McIntosh was eventually moved to a military cemetery. The remaining five who died were lost in a mass burial grave. There is no indication whether or not any of the Canadians at Little Bighorn who lived to tell the tale ever returned to their home country.

When the steamer *Far West* pulled in to Bismarck, Dakota Territory, and Clement Lounsberry, editor of the *Bismark Tribune* newspaper, learned of the defeat of Custer's command, he worked through the night to put out a special rush edition. On July 6, 1876, the *Bismarck Tribune* published the *Tribune Extra*, running with the banner line, "First Account of the Custer Massacre."

Lounsberry, who had, fortunately for him, been unable to accompany Custer and had sent his correspondent Mark Kellogg, wrote a lengthy article full of flowery speech chronicling the battle. He commented on the fact Kellogg's body was left intact, not mutilated like the others. "Perhaps as they [the Indians] had learned to respect the great Chief Custer and for that reason did not mutilate his remains they had in like manner learned to respect this humble shover of the lead pencil and to that fact can be attributed this result."[1] Probably Kellogg was left untouched simply because he was among the first killed in Custer's command and his body was far from the others. In fact the troopers didn't spot it until they were leaving the battle site. Lounsberry's far-fetched thinking can be attributed to emotion and the writing style of the day.

Lounsberry also telegraphed the news, including Kellogg's earlier correspondence, to a number of eastern newspapers, including the *New York Herald*. Two letters written by Kellogg were published posthumously by the *Herald* on July 11, 1876.

Some of Kellogg's diary and notes that survived are in the possession of the North Dakota State Historical Society and are a source of information on the days preceding the battle.

Custer's body was found with two bullet holes: one at the left temple, and one above the heart. He and his brother Tom were covered with pieces of tent canvas and blankets, and buried side by side on the battlefield. One year later Custer's body was exhumed and sent east. On October 10, 1877, he was reburied with full military honours in West Point Cemetery, at the military academy where he did so poorly in life.

Custer certainly won fame after the battle at the Little Bighorn, but also received his fair share of criticism. One of his critics was President Ulysses S. Grant, who never forgave Custer for his criticism of the government. On September 1, 1876, the *New York Herald* quoted Grant: "I regard Custer's Massacre as a sacrifice of troops, brought on by Custer himself that was wholly unnecessary — wholly unnecessary."[2]

Meanwhile, his former leader, General Philip Sheridan, noted Custer's three military blunders: at Powder River refusing General Terry's offer of an additional four companies of the Second Cavalry (this might have included MacAdams in the fight); he left the Gatling guns on the *Far West*, even though he knew he was facing superior numbers; on the day of the battle Custer divided his 600-man command.

Years later, General Nelson A. Miles, who became the army's most renowned Indian fighter after Custer's death, wrote of the battle that no commander can win "with seven-twelfths of the command remaining out of the engagement when within sound of his rifle shots."[3] That implied the other cavalry companies intentionally ignored their comrades in Custer's command who were in distress.

Widow Elizabeth "Libbie" Custer did her best to polish her husband's image after his death. She launched a one-woman campaign, including speaking engagements, with that in mind. She wrote three books: *Boots and Saddle* in 1885, *Following the Guidon* in 1890, and *Tenting on the Plains* in 1893. These were all slanted in her husband's favour, creating him as a hero gallantly leading his men into battle.

Elizabeth Custer died in New York City, April 4, 1933, just short of her ninety-first birthday. Although she had been hard-pressed for money when her husband died, she left an estate of $100,000 in 1933. Many eye-witnesses at the battle of the Little Bighorn had withheld their stories out of respect for Libbie Custer, waiting for her to die, but she outlived most of them. And only fifty years after her death did historians begin taking a closer look at Custer and Custer's Last Stand.

Major Marcus Reno's reputation suffered following reports of the battle. He was assigned to a far-off post where he was eventually charged in connection with his unwanted advances toward another officer's wife. A court martial found him guilty and he was suspended without pay for two years. Reno's drinking continued. In a bid to clear his name over the battle at the Little Bighorn, he requested an investigation. A court of enquiry, not a court martial, was established at the headquarters of the army division of Missouri in Chicago.

The enquiry opened January 13, 1879. There were twenty-three witnesses. As they testified, some trying to protect their own reputations and the glory of the Seventh Cavalry, it seemed that the enquiry was not just investigating Reno's actions but assigning blame for the massacre. One question in play was the fact of Reno leaving his troopers behind in the woods while he took to the hill, instead of providing action against that side of the Indian village.

Reno took the stand. "I had known General Custer a long time and I had no confidence in his ability as a soldier."[4] When asked what became of the wounded men in the woods and those left at the river crossing, Reno answered, "I do not know, the Indians would not permit me to take care of them."[5]

The defence upheld the honour of the officers' testimony as compared to the lower status witnesses. The prosecution held that Reno contributed to Custer's defeat by not holding the woods and attacking the village from there, and that his seven companies had not supported Custer. Despite it all Reno was found innocent. The Seventh had closed ranks. Reno returned to active duty in six weeks but his life was on a downward slope.

In 1880 he was court martialled a second time, this time for drunkenness, and dismissed from service. He worked as a civil servant in Washington, D.C., and died March 30, 1889, at the age of fifty-four. He was buried in Washington, but years later, in 1967, a descendant lobbied successfully to have Reno's body re-interred in the Custer National Cemetery on the Little Bighorn battlefield.

Months after the battle of Little Bighorn, Sitting Bull crossed the Canadian border with his band, taking the Hunkpapas to Wood Mountain, Saskatchewan. There he stayed for about four years. In

1881 he returned to the United States, to Standing Rock Indian Reserve in the Dakotas. For a while the chief toured as a performer in the Buffalo Bill Cody Wild West Show.

The Sioux were suffering, losing some of the reservation lands, going hungry from reduced rations at the agencies, and from bad crops. A new faith arose in the form of a Paiute holy man and a new religion the whites called the Ghost Dance. Believers thought that dancing the Ghost Dance through the winter would bring better conditions the next spring. The Indian agent at Standing Rock feared that Sitting Bull would further influence what was considered by the whites to be a "subversive" movement.

On December 15, 1890, the agent ordered Sitting Bull arrested. During the ensuing struggle, one of Sitting Bull's supporters fired on police. The reserve Indian police officer shot Sitting Bull, killing him; he was fifty-nine years old. His body was taken to nearby Fort Yates for burial. In 1953, remains thought to be his were exhumed and buried at McBridge, South Dakota, by the Lakota Sioux. Not everyone agreed this was Sitting Bull's body.

The Oglala warrior Crazy Horse had fought to preserve the land and traditions of his Lakota way of life; a losing battle. In February of 1877, in the government's Black Hills Act, all of Paha Sapa, the Black Hills, along with nearly twenty-three million acres of surrounding territory, were taken over by the U.S. government; in exchange, the Indians received rations for an indefinite period. Crazy Horse seemed to realize the hopelessness of his situation, and thinking he would at least get a reservation for his people, finally surrendered to U.S. troops. He arrived at the Red Cloud agency near Camp Robinson in what is now Nebraska, on May 5, that same year, less than one year after the battle of Little Bighorn, and settled in a nearby village. There was growing trouble from two sides. Other Indians, such as Oglala Chief Red Cloud, were jealous of the attention Crazy Horse was getting; the military wanted him to help them fight other Indian bands.

The great warrior never received the Powder River reservation offered by General Crook; once Crazy Horse led his warriors into captivity, the U.S. government forgot its offer. "Crazy Horse foresaw the consequence of his surrender. It meant submission to a people who he did not consider his equal; it meant the doom of his race."[6]

General George Crook, the same General Crook who never did show up at the Little Bighorn, was ordered to Camp Robinson. When Crook was told, wrongly apparently, that Crazy Horse had threatened to kill him, he ordered the warrior arrested. Crazy Horse fled; then returned to the military camp. When he realized he was heading for jail, Crazy Horse struggled to get out of the guardhouse.

> The windows were barred with iron, and he could see men behind the bars with chains on their legs. It was a trap for an animal, and Crazy Horse lunged away like a trapped animal, with Little Big Man holding on to his arm. The scuffling went on for only a few seconds. Someone shouted a command, and then the soldier guard, Private William Gentles, thrust his bayonet deep into Crazy Horse's abdomen.[7]

The Oglala warrior died that night, September 5, 1877. Crazy Horse's body was turned over to his elderly parents who took it to Camp Sheridan and put it on a traditional scaffold. The parents later moved it to an unknown location. A monument was dedicated to Crazy Horse and a memorial was carved in the Black Hills similar to the one of U.S. presidents at Mount Rushmore. This was a controversial move among the Lakota Sioux since the Black Hills were considered sacred land.

In 1890 the Seventh Cavalry became embroiled in another controversial incident with the Indians — the massacre at Wounded Knee, Dakota Territory. None of the Canadians with Custer in 1876 were still with the cavalry at the time. It was no secret the Seventh felt it had a score to settle with the Indians stemming from the battle of Little Bighorn fourteen years earlier.

On December 23, 1890, Chief Big Foot led his band of 350 Minneconjou Sioux from the Cheyenne Agency, on the way to join Oglala Chief Red Cloud. Five days later the Seventh Cavalry came upon them east of Pine Ridge in the valley of Wounded Knee Creek in what is now South Dakota. The Indians, their chief ill with pneumonia, surrendered.

The Seventh, with about 500 troops, set up camp on a square with soldiers camped on three sides. The Indians pitched their camp nearby, Big Foot retiring to his tent because of illness. Major James Forsyth had decided to disarm the Indians and ship them to Omaha until the Ghost Dance trouble passed.

On December 29, 120 Minniconjou warriors gathered to be disarmed. A painted medicine man jumped up doing the Ghost Dance and told them to resist. As the gun search continued, one young warrior raised his rifle and shot in the air. This prompted the troopers to begin firing into the warriors. It was chaos as the troopers fired not only into the Indians but into their comrades across the square. Big Foot was shot as he lay on his pallet, and his daughter was killed as well. Captain Godfrey was ordered to take twenty men to look for fleeing Indians. They shot into a bush and killed a woman and three children.

After troopers headed out for Pine Ridge agency with the wounded cavalrymen, soldiers gathered up the remaining Indians and loaded them into wagons. It was apparent by the end of the day that a blizzard was approaching, so the dead Indians were left lying where they had fallen. The wagonloads of Sioux reached Pine Ridge after dark. They were left lying in the open until the Episcopal mission was opened, benches taken out, and hay scattered over the rough flooring. "... above the pulpit was strung a crudely lettered banner: PEACE ON EARTH, GOOD WILL TO MEN."[8]

At Wounded Knee that day, 172 Sioux died — more than sixty of them women and children. The cavalry lost twenty-five dead and thirty-nine were wounded, most of them struck by their own bullets or shrapnel.

Newspapers carried the story. One newspaper reported, "It was a war of extermination now with the troopers.... There was only one common impulse — to kill wherever an Indian could be seen," including old men and women, mothers, and small children."[9]

Three days later, on January 1, 1891, a contractor was paid two dollars a body to bury the frozen bodies in a mass grave. A court hearing exonerated Forsyth of any faulty disposition of his troops, and the entire regiment of any indiscriminate killing of women and children. A later military report indicated that "the dead women and children killed by Godfrey's men all had distinct powder burns on them, indicating deliberate execution from point-blank range."[10]

The massacre of Indian men, women, and children at Wounded Knee, Dakota, was a final blow to the American Native peoples' life as they knew it on the western plains.

They made us many promises, more than I can remember, but they never kept but one; they promised to take our land, and they took it.[11]

— Chief Red Cloud, in old age, 1882

NOTES

PROLOGUE

1. Dee Brown, *Bury My Heart at Wounded Knee: An Indian History of the American West* (New York: Holt, Rinehart & Winston, 1970), 5.

2. *Ibid.*, 8.

CHAPTER 1

1. Lawrence A. Frost, *The Court-Martial of General George Armstrong Custer.* (Norman, Oklahoma: University of Oklahoma, 1968), 63.

2. E. L. Reedstrom, *Bugles, Banners and War Bonnets* (Caldwell, Idaho: Caxton Printers Ltd., 1977), 35.

3. Frost, *The Court-Martial of General George Armstrong Custer*, 75.

4. United States Senate and House Documents. 40th Congress, 3rd Session, 1868/1869. Document No. 1, 35.

CHAPTER 2

1. *The Custer Story*, edited by Marguerite Merington (New York: Barnes and Noble, 1994), 159.

CHAPTER 3

1. Lawrence A. Frost, *The Court-Martial of General George Armstrong Custer.* (Norman, Oklahoma: University of Oklahoma, 1968), 99–100.

2. *Ibid.*, 101.

3. "Proceedings of a General Court Martial, Special Orders 426, War Department, Adjutant General's Office, August 27, 1867," Lawrence A. Frost Collection, Monroe County Library George Armstrong Custer Collection, 16.

4. *Ibid.*, 23.

5. *Ibid.*, 31–32.

6. *Ibid.*, 33.

7. *Ibid.*, 38.

8. *Ibid.*, 58.

9. *Ibid.*, 63–64.

10. *The Custer Story*, edited by Marguerite Merington (New York: Barnes and Noble, 1994), 211–12.

11. *Proceedings of a General Court Martial*, 83.

12. *Ibid.*, 89.

CHAPTER 4

1. "Proceedings of a General Court Martial, Special Orders 426, War Department, Adjutant General's Office, August 27, 1867," Lawrence A. Frost Collection, Monroe County Library George Armstrong Custer Collection, 12.

2. *Ibid.*, 13.

3. *Ibid.*, 112–13.

4. *Ibid.*, 14–15.

5. *General Court Martial*, 126.

6. *Exhibits and Findings*, 51.

7. *The Custer Story*, edited by Marguerite Merington (New York: Barnes and Noble, 1994), 214.

8. Lawrence A. Frost, *The Court-Martial of General George Armstrong Custer*. (Norman, Oklahoma: University of Oklahoma, 1968), 261.

9. *Ibid.*, 264.

10. *Ibid.*, 266.

11. Merington, *The Custer Story*, 217.

CHAPTER 5

1. Dr. Sharon Jaeger, *The Work of Our Hands: A History of Mount Pleasant, 1799–1899* (Mount Pleasant, Ontario: Heritage Mount Pleasant, 2004), 141.

2. *Ibid.*, 193.

3. *Ibid.*, 19.

CHAPTER 6

1. Donald McIntosh Sr., "Letter to his Sister Christy McIntosh, Cornwall, Upper Canada, August 12, 1816." Fur Trade Collection, F 431, Archives of Ontario.

2. James Willert, "The Wedding Ring of Lieutenant Donald McIntosh: DISCOVERED?" *Research Review Journal of the little Big Horn Associates*, Vol. 10, No. 2, June 1996, 5.

3. *Ibid.*, 6.

4. *Ibid.*, 6.

5. *Ibid.*, 7.

6. Katherine Gibson Fougera, *With Custer's Cavalry* (Caldwell, Idaho: Caxton Printers, Ltd., 1940), 68.

7. *Ibid.*, 60.

8. *Ibid.*, 139.

CHAPTER 7

1. United States Senate and House Documents. 40th Congress, 3rd Session, 1868/1869, Document No. 13, 22.

2. *The Custer Story*, edited by Marguerite Merington (New York: Barnes and Noble, 1994), 199.

3. G.A. Custer, *My Life on the Plains*, ed. Milo Milton Quaife (Lincoln, Nebraska: University of Nebraska Press, 1966).

4. *Ibid.*, 268.

5. Merington, *The Custer Story*, 222.

6. *Ibid.*, 223.

CHAPTER 8

1. *General Custer and the Battle of Washita: The Federal View*, edited by John Carroll (Byran, Texas: Guidon Press, 1978), 80. 41st Congress, 2nd Session, House of Representatives Executive Document No. 240.

2. *Ibid.*, 53. 40th Congress, 3rd Session, Senate Executive Document No. 18.

3. *Ibid.*, 81. 41st Congress, 2nd Session, House of Representatives Executive Document No. 240.

4. *Ibid.*, 253.

5. *Ibid.*, 87.

6. *Ibid.*, 86.

7. *Ibid.*, 228

CHAPTER 9

1. Evan S. Connell, *Son of the Morning Star* (San Francisco: North Point Press, 1984), 149.

2. Letter to Libbie Custer from Anna Darragh, October 1864. Monroe County Historical Museum.

3. Marian Childs, *Reflections of Life in Monroe County, Michigan, 1952–62*. Unpublished document, Collection of the Monroe County Library System, 1962, 420.

4. Dixon, D, "The Sordid Side of the 7ᵗʰ Cavalry," *Little Bighorn Associates Research Review*, 1 (1) New Series, June 1987.

5. *The Custer Story*, edited by Marguerite Merington (New York: Barnes and Noble, 1994), 232

6. Custer, George A., *My Life on the Plains*, ed. Milo Milton Quaife (Chicago: Lakeside Press, R.R. Donnelley & Sons Co., 1952), xxxvii.

7. *Ibid.*, xli.

8. *Ibid.*, xlii.

9. *Ibid.*, 512.

10. *Ibid.*, 515.

11. *Ibid.*, 595.

12. *Ibid.*, 596.

CHAPTER 10

1. Steve Arnold and Tim French, *Custer's Forgotten Friend: The Life of William Winer Cooke*, (Hamilton: self-published, 1993), 18.

2. *Ibid.*, 17, 18.

3. James Willert, "The Wedding Ring of Lieutenant Donald McIntosh: DISCOVERED?" *Research Review Journal of the little Big Horn Associates*, Vol. 10, No. 2, June 1996, 7.

4. Lieutenant Donald McIntosh's diary from 1872 to 1876. Transcribed by Lieutenant-Colonel (Retired) Daniel O.

Magnussen. Collection of the Battlefield National Monument Museum, Montana.

5. Register of Enlistments, United States Army, 1863.

6. James E. Heitland, "1st Lieutenant Donald McIntosh, (Custer's Forgotten Clansman...)," *www.us7thcavcof.com/Dedication.html*.

7. Katherine Gibson Fougera, *With Custer's Cavalry* (Caldwell, Idaho: Caxton Printers, Ltd., 1940), 13.

CHAPTER 11

1. M. John Lubetkin, *Jay Cooke's Gamble: The Northern Pacific Railroad, the Sioux, and the Panic of 1873* (Norman, Oklahoma: University of Oklahoma Press, 2006), 80.

2. Gregory J.W. Urwin, *Custer Victorious* (Toronto: Associated University Presses, 1983), 163.

3. *The Custer Story*, edited by Marguerite Merington (New York: Barnes and Noble, 1994), 104.

4. Lubetkin, *Jay Cooke's Gamble*, 129.

CHAPTER 12

1. James R. Gai, "Felix Vinatieri: A Biography," *The Journal of the Little Big Horn Associates*, Vol. 2, No 1, June 1988, 16–26.

2. *The Custer Story*, edited by Marguerite Merington (New York: Barnes and Noble, 1994), 249.

3. *Ibid.*, 252.

4. *Ibid.*, 256.

5. James Willert, "The Wedding Ring of Lieutenant Donald McIntosh: DISCOVERED?" *Research Review Journal of the little Big Horn Associates*, Vol. 10, No. 2, June 1996, 7.

6. Merington, *The Custer Story*, 261.

7. M. John Lubetkin, *Jay Cooke's Gamble: The Northern Pacific Railroad, the Sioux, and the Panic of 1873* (Norman, Oklahoma: University of Oklahoma Press, 2006), 286.

CHAPTER 13

1. *The Custer Story*, edited by Marguerite Merington (New York: Barnes and Noble, 1994), 60.

2. *Ibid.*, 68.

3. *Ibid.*, 74.

CHAPTER 14

1. Charles A. Eastman, *Indian Heroes and Great Chieftains.* (Lincoln and London, Nebraska: University of Nebraska Press, 1991), 16.

2. *Ibid.*, 79.

3. *Ibid.*, 81.

4. Peter Matthiessen, *In the Spirit of Crazy Horse* (New York: Viking Press, 1983), 10.

5. Eastman, *Indian Heroes and Great Chieftains*, 117.

6. *Ibid.*, 120.

7. Frederick J. Chiaventone, "Red Cloud's War: The Fetterman Massacre," *Cowboys and Indians Magazine*, April, 2009. *www.cowboysindians.com/Cowboys-Indians/April-2009/Red-Clouds-War-The-Fetterman-Massacre.*

8. *Ibid.*

9. Edward Lazarus, *Black Hills White Justice: The Sioux Nation Versus the United States, 1775 to the Present* (New York: Harper Collins Publishers, 1991), 46.

10. "Treaty with the Sioux-Brule, Oglala, Miniconjou, Yanktonai, Hunkpapa, Blakfee, Cuthead, Two Kettle, Sans Arcs, and

Santee — and Arapaho," *The Sioux Treaty of 1868*, Article 16, 1868, 433.

11. Eastman, *Indian Heroes and Great Chieftains*, 118.

12. Lazarus, *Black Hills White Justice*, 60.

13. "The 1874 Custer Expedition to the Black Hills," *Visitor Magazine*. www.blackhillsvisitor.com/main.asp?id=14&cat_id=30136.

CHAPTER 15

1. M. John Lubetkin, *Jay Cooke's Gamble: The Northern Pacific Railroad, the Sioux, and the Panic of 1873* (Norman, Oklahoma: University of Oklahoma Press, 2006), 276.

2. *Ibid.*, 277.

3. *Ibid.*, 283.

4. *The Custer Story*, edited by Marguerite Merington (New York: Barnes and Noble, 1994), 271.

5. William Ludlow, *Report of a Reconnaissance of the Black Hills of Dakota, The Summer of 1874* (Washington, D.C.: Government Printing Office, 1875).

6. Katherine Gibson Fougera, *With Custer's Cavalry* (Caldwell, Idaho: Caxton Printers, Ltd., 1940), 103.

7. Dr. Brian Dippie, "It's Equal I Have Never Seen: Custer Explores the Black Hills in 1874," *Columbia: The Magazine of the Northwest History* (Summer 2005): 19.

CHAPTER 16

1. Dr. Brian Dippie, "It's Equal I Have Never Seen: Custer Explores the Black Hills in 1874," *Columbia: The Magazine of the Northwest History* (Summer 2005): 21.

2. *The Custer Story*, edited by Marguerite Merington (New York: Barnes and Noble, 1994), 272

3. *Ibid.*, 273.

4. Dippie, "It's Equal I Have Never Seen," 25.

5. *Ibid.*, 26.

CHAPTER 17

1. Katherine Gibson Fougera, *With Custer's Cavalry* (Caldwell, Idaho: Caxton Printers, Ltd., 1940), 189.

2. *Ibid.*, 193.

3. *Ibid.*, 196.

4. *Ibid.*, 208.

CHAPTER 18

1. Edward Lazarus, *Black Hills White Justice: The Sioux Nation Versus the United States, 1775 to the Present* (New York: Harper Collins Publishers, 1991), 81.

2. *Ibid.*, 83.

3. Joan Chetwynd, "Yarmouth in the Eighteen Hundreds," First Prize, Yarmouth Centennial Essay Contest, Grade 10, Yarmouth Memorial High School, *The Yarmouth Herald*, May 1960.

4. Brian Medel, "Two Canadians Who Fought at Little Big Horn," the *Halifax Herald*, Nova Scotia, June 24, 2005.

5. Bernie and Stephen Rosevear, *Canadians with Custer in 1876* (Monroe, Michigan: Monroe County Library System, 1992) 13–18.

6. Lewis O. Saum, *Colonel Custer's Copperhead: The "Mysterious" Mark Kellogg*, a publication of the Montana Historical Society, Vol. XXVIII, No. 4, October 1978, 15.

7. *Ibid.*, 17.

8. *Ibid.*, 12.

9. *Ibid.*, 20.

CHAPTER 19

1. Lieutenant Donald McIntosh's diary from 1872 to 1876. Transcribed by Lieutenant-Colonel (Retired) Daniel O. Magnussen. Collection of the Battlefield National Monument, Montana, 88–90.

2. *Ibid.*

CHAPTER 20

1. *The Custer Story*, edited by Marguerite Merington (New York: Barnes and Noble, 1994), 277.

2. *Ibid.*, 287.

3. *Ibid.*, 292.

4. James Donovan, *A Terrible Glory* (New York: Little, Brown and Company, 2008), 114.

5. Evan S. Connell, *Son of the Morning Star* (New York: Harper Collins Publishers, 1985), 106.

6. Peter Matthiessen, *In the Spirit of Crazy Horse* (New York: Viking Press, 1983), 11.

7. Connell, *Son of the Morning Star*, 83–85.

8. Donovan, *A Terrible Glory*, 133.

9. Connell, *Son of the Morning Star*, 93.

CHAPTER 21

1. James Donovan, *A Terrible Glory* (New York: Little, Brown and Company, 2008), 135.

2. *Ibid.*, 118.

3. *Ibid.*, 123.

4. Bernie and Stephen Rosevear, *Canadians with Custer in 1876* (Monroe, Michigan: Monroe County Library System, 1992) 20.

5. Mark Kellogg, *Notes of the Little Big Horn Expedition Under General Custer, 1876.* Historical Society of Montana, Vol. IX, (Boston, Massachusetts: J.S. Canner and Company, Inc., 1966), 213.

6. *Ibid.*, 214.

7. *Ibid.*, 215.

8. *Ibid.*, 216.

9. *The Custer Story*, edited by Marguerite Merington (New York: Barnes and Noble, 1994), 300.

10. Donovan, *A Terrible Glory*, 145.

11. *Ibid.*, 146.

CHAPTER 22

1. Evan S. Connell, *Son of the Morning Star* (New York: Harper Collins Publishers, 1985), 267.

2. James Donovan, *A Terrible Glory* (New York: Little, Brown and Company, 2008), 149.

3. Mark Kellogg, *Notes of the Little Big Horn Expedition Under General Custer, 1876.* Historical Society of Montana, Vol. IX, (Boston, Massachusetts: J.S. Canner and Company, Inc., 1966), 221.

4. *Ibid.*, 222.

5. *The Custer Story*, edited by Marguerite Merington (New York: Barnes and Noble, 1994), p 302.

6. *Ibid.*, 305.

7. Merington, *The Custer Story*, 309.

8. Katherine Gibson Fougera, *With Custer's Cavalry* (Caldwell, Idaho: Caxton Printers, Ltd., 1940), 277.

9. Colonel W.A. Graham, *The Custer Myth: A Source Book of Custerania.* (Harrisburg, Pennsylvania: The Stackpole Co., 1953), 233–35.

10. Connell, *Son of the Morning Star*, 299.

11. Merington, *The Custer Story*, 307.

12. *Ibid.*, 308.

CHAPTER 23

1. James Donovan, *A Terrible Glory* (New York: Little, Brown and Company, 2008), 191.

2. *Ibid.*, 193.

3. Evan S. Connell, *Son of the Morning Star* (New York: Harper Collins Publishers, 1985), 261.

4. Donovan, *A Terrible Glory*, 198.

CHAPTER 24

1. James Donovan, *A Terrible Glory* (New York: Little, Brown and Company, 2008), 211.

2. Evan S. Connell, *Son of the Morning Star* (New York: Harper Collins Publishers, 1985), 278.

3. Donovan, *A Terrible Glory*, 215.

4. *Ibid.*, 217.

CHAPTER 25

1. James Donovan, *A Terrible Glory* (New York: Little, Brown and Company, 2008), 235.

2. Richard G. Hardorff, *Lakota Recollections of the Custer Fight.* Lincoln, Nebraska: University of Nebraska Press, 1997, 40.

3. Donovan, *A Terrible Glory,* 240.

4. James Willert, "The Wedding Ring of Lieutenant Donald McIntosh: DISCOVERED?" *Research Review Journal of the little Big Horn Associates,* Vol. 10, No. 2, June 1996, 9.

5. *Ibid.*

6. *Ibid.*

7. Dee Brown, *Bury My Heart at Wounded Knee: An Indian History of the American West* (New York: Holt, Rinehart & Winston, 1970), 294.

8. Donovan, *A Terrible Glory,* 248.

9. Bernie and Stephen Rosevear, *Canadians with Custer in 1876* (Monroe, Michigan: Monroe County Library System, 1992), 15.

10. Gregory F. Michno, *Lakota Noon: The Indian Narrative of Custer's Defeat* (Missoula, Montana: Mountain Press Publishing Company, 1997), 115.

11. *Ibid.,* 155.

CHAPTER 26

1. Letter by Robert Newton Price, 1879. (former classmate of Lieutenant Benjamin Hodgson at West Point). Collection number SC 1005, folder 1/1. Montana Historical Society, North Roberts, Helena, Montana. USA. 59620-1201

2. James Donovan, *A Terrible Glory* (New York: Little, Brown and Company, 2008), 257.

3. *Ibid.*, 259.

4. Gregory F. Michno, *Lakota Noon: The Indian Narrative of Custer's Defeat* (Missoula, Montana: Mountain Press Publishing Company, 1997), 165.

5. *Ibid.*, 198.

6. Donovan, *A Terrible Glory*, 271.

7. *Ibid.*, 276.

8. Richard G. Hardorff, *Lakota Recollections of the Custer Fight.* Lincoln, Nebraska: University of Nebraska Press, 1997, 75–76, 86–88.

CHAPTER 27

1. Richard G. Hardorff, *Lakota Recollections of the Custer Fight.* Lincoln, Nebraska: University of Nebraska Press, 1997, 66.

2. James Donovan, *A Terrible Glory* (New York: Little, Brown and Company, 2008), 276.

3. Evan S. Connell, *Son of the Morning Star* (New York: Harper Collins Publishers, 1985), 289.

4. Donovan, *A Terrible Glory*, 286.

5. *Ibid.*, 292.

CHAPTER 28

1. Evan S. Connell, *Son of the Morning Star* (New York: Harper Collins Publishers, 1985), 286.

2. Statistics. Little Bighorn Battlefield National Monument.

3. James Donovan, *A Terrible Glory* (New York: Little, Brown and Company, 2008), 305.

4. Richard G. Hardorff, *Lakota Recollections of the Custer Fight.* Lincoln, Nebraska: University of Nebraska Press, 1997, 66.

5. *The Custer Story*, edited by Marguerite Merington (New York: Barnes and Noble, 1994), 323.

CHAPTER 29

1. Steve Arnold and Tim French, *Custer's Forgotten Friend: The Life of William Winer Cooke*, (Hamilton: self-published, 1993), 35–36.

2. *Ibid.*, 37.

3. James Willert, "The Wedding Ring of Lieutenant Donald McIntosh: DISCOVERED?" *Research Review Journal of the little Big Horn Associates*, Vol. 10, No. 2, June 1996, 9.

4. Richard G. Hardorff, *The Custer Battle Casualties: Burials, Exhumations, and Reinterments* (El Segundo, California: Upton and Sons, Publishers, 1989), 132.

5. *Ibid.*

6. Katherine Gibson Fougera, *With Custer's Cavalry* (Caldwell, Idaho: Caxton Printers, Ltd., 1940), 271–72.

7. Hardorff, *The Custer Battle Casualties*, 134.

8. Fougera, *With Custer's Cavalry*, 277.

9. *The Battlefield Dispatch*, Vol. 14, No. 2, Spring, 1995.

10. Mr. Pierce, Committee on Pensions. 51st Congress, 1st Session, Senate of the United States, Report No. 1439, July 2, 1890.

CHAPTER 30

1. United States Army pension application file index card. Vickory John (alias), Groesbeck, John H.

2. *The Yarmouth Herald*, deaths column, December 7, 1876.

3. Bernie and Stephen Rosevear, *Canadians with Custer in 1876* (Monroe, Michigan: Monroe County Library System, 1992) 14.

4. Richard G. Hardorff, *The Custer Battle Casualties: Burials, Exhumations, and Reinterments* (El Segundo, California: Upton and Sons, Publishers, 1989), 122.

5. Bernie and Stephen Rosevear, *Canadians with Custer in 1876* (Monroe, Michigan: Monroe County Library System, 1992) 14.

6. *Ibid.*, 16.

7. *Ibid.*, 18.

EPILOGUE

1. "First Account of the Custer Massacre," *Bismarck Dakota Tribune, Tribune Extra.* July 6, 1876. *http://genealogytrails.com/main/military/battleoflittlebighorn.html.*

2. "Mark Kellogg's Last Letter," the *New York Herald,* July 11, 1876. *http://www.astonisher.com/archives/museum/mark_kellogg_big_horn.html.*

3. Louise Barnett, *Touched by Fire* (New York: Henry Holt and Company, 1996), 311.

4. Major Marcus A. Reno, "The Official Record of a Court of Inquiry Convened at Chicago, Illinois, January 13, 1879, by the President of the United States Upon the Request of Major Marcus A. Reno, 7th U.S. Cavalry, to investigate his conduct at the Battle of the Little Big Horn, June 25-26, 1876," University of Wisconsin Digital Collections. *http://digicoll.library.wisc.edu/cgi-bin/History/History-idx?type=turn&entity=History.Reno.p0546&id=History.Reno&isize=M.*

5. *Ibid.*

6. Peter Matthiessen, *In the Spirit of Crazy Horse* (New York: Viking Press, 1983), 14.

7. Dee Brown, *Bury My Heart at Wounded Knee: An Indian History of the American West* (New York: Holt, Rinehart & Winston, 1970), 312.

8. *Ibid.*, 445.

9. James Donovan, *A Terrible Glory* (New York: Little, Brown and Company, 2008), 392.

10. *Ibid.*, 393.

11. Brown, *Bury My Heart at Wounded Knee*, 448.

BIBLIOGRAPHY

Arnold, Steve and Tim French. *Custer's Forgotten Friend: The life of W.W. Cooke*. Hamilton: Self-published, 1993.

Barnett, Louise K. *Touched by Fire: The Life, Death, and Mythic Afterlife of George Armstrong Custer*. New York: Henry Holt and Company, 1996.

Boyle, Terry. *Hidden Ontario*. Polar Bear Press, Toronto, 1999.

Brown, Dee. *Bury My Heart at Wounded Knee: An Indian History of the American West*. New York: Holt, Rinehart & Winston, 1970.

Capps, Benjamin. *The Great Chiefs*. New York: Time Inc., 1975.

Carroll, John Editor. *General Custer and the Battle of the Washita: The Federal View*. Bryan, Texas: Guidon Press, 1978.

Churchill, Ward and Jim Vander Wall. *Agents of Repression*. Cambridge, Massachusetts: South End Press, 2002.

Connell, Evan. *Son of the Morning Star*. San Francisco: North Point Press, 1984.

Custer, General George A. *My Life on the Plains*. Ed. Milo Milton Quaife. Chicago: The Lakeside Press, R.R. Donnelley & Sons Co., 1952.

_____. *My Life on the Plains*. Ed. Milo Milton Quaife. Lincoln, Nebraska: University of Nebraska Press, 1966.

The Custer Story: The Life and Letters of General George A. Custer and His Wife Elizabeth. Marguerite Merington, editor. New York: Barnes & Noble Books, 1994.

Donovan, James. *A Terrible Glory*. New York: Little, Brown and Company, 2008.

Eastman, Charles A. *Indian Heroes and Great Chieftains*. Lincoln, Nebraska: University of Nebraska Press, 1991.

Fougera, Katherine Gibson. *With Custer's Cavalry*. Caldwell, Idaho: The Caxton Printers, Ltd., 1940.

Freeman, Bill. *Hamilton A People's History*. Toronto: James Lorimer & Co., 2001.

Frost, Lawrence. A. *The Court-Martial of General George Armstrong Custer*. Norman, Oklahoma: University of Oklahoma Press, 1968.

Graham, Colonel W.A. *The Custer Myth: A Source Book of Custerania*. Harrisburg, Pennsylvania: The Stackpole Co., 1953.

Hardorff, Richard G. *Lakota Recollections of the Custer Fight: New Sources of Indian-Military History*. Lincoln, Nebraska: University of Nebraska Press, 1997.

_____. *The Custer Battle Casualties Burials, Exhumations, and Reinterments*. El Segundo, California: Upton and Sons, Publishers, 1989.

Hoy, Claire. *Canadians in the Civil War*. Toronto: McArthur and Company, 2004.

Jaeger, Dr. Sharon. *The Work of Our Hands: A History of Mount Pleasant, 1799–1899*. Mount Pleasant, Ontario: Heritage Mount Pleasant, 2004.

Lazarus, Edward. *Black Hills White Justice: The Sioux Nation Versus the United States, 1775 to the Present*. New York: Harper Collins Publishers, 1991.

Lubetkin, M. John. *Jay Cooke's Gamble: The Northern Pacific Railroad, the Sioux, and the Panic of 1873*. Norman, Oklahoma: University of Oklahoma Press, 2006.

Matthiessen, Peter. *In the Spirit of Crazy Horse.* New York: The Viking Press, 1983.

Mcmurtry, Larry. *O What A Slaughter: Massacres in the American West 1846–1890.* New York: Simon and Schuster, 2005.

Michno, Gregory F. *Lakota Noon: The Indian Narrative of Custer's Defeat.* Missoula, Montana: Mountain Press Publishing Company, 1997.

Reedstrom, Ernest Lisle. *Bugles, Banners, and War Bonnets.* Caldwell, Idaho: The Caxton Printers Ltd., 1977.

Saum, Lewis O. *Colonel Custer's Copperhead: The "Mysterious" Mark Kellogg.* Publication of The Montana Historical Society, Volume XXVIII, Number Four, October, 1978.

Urwin, Gregory J.W. *Custer Victorious.* Toronto: Associated University Press, 1983.

ARCHIVES

House of Representatives, 51st Congress, 2nd Session, January 13, 1891, Report no. 3453.

Kellogg, Marcus (Mark) Henry. *Notes of the Little Big Horn Expedition Under General Custer, 1876.* Transcribed. The Historical Society of Montana.

Ludlow, William. *Report of a Reconnaissance of the Black Hills of Dakota, Made in the Summer of 1874.* Monroe County Library System, Lawrence A. Frost Collection. Washington: Government Printing Office, 1875.

McIntosh, Donald Sr. *Letter to His Sister Christy McIntosh, Cornwall, Upper Canada, August 12, 1816.* Toronto: Archives of Ontario.

McIntosh, Lieutenant Donald's diary from 1872 to 1876. Transcribed by Lieutenant-Colonel (Retired) Daniel O. Magnussen. Collection of the Battlefield National Monument, Montana.

Montana Historical Society, Volume IX, J.S. Canner and Company Inc. Boston Mass. 1966.

Montana Historical Society, Volume XXVIII, J.S. Canner and Company Inc, Boston Mass. 1978.

"Paris Man Survives Custer's Last Stand." *The Paris Star*, July 22, 1976, 3.

Proceedings of a General Court Martial, Special Orders 426, War Department, Adjutant General's Office, August 27, 1867. Monroe County Library System, George Armstrong Custer Collection.

Senate of the United States, 51st Congress, 1st Session, July 2, 1890, Report No. 1439.

Treaty with the Sioux — Brule, Oglala, Miniconjou, Yanktonai, Hunkpapa, Blackfeet, Cuthead, Two Kettle, Sans Arcs, and Santee — and Arapaho, 1868. Article 16. Black Hills White Justice. Monroe County Library System, Ellis Reference and Information Center, Lawrence A. Frost Collection,

United States Army. Pension application file index card: Vickory, John (alias), Groesbeck, John H.

United States Army. Register of Enlistments, 1866, 1869, 1874.

United States Senate and House Documents, 40th Congress, 3rd Session, 1868–1869, Document No. 13.

MAGAZINES AND NEWSPAPERS

Dippie, Dr. Brian W. "It's Equal I Have Never Seen: Custer Explores the Black Hills in 1874," *Columbia: The Magazine of the Northwest History*, (Summer 2005), 18–27.

Medel, Brian. "Two Canadians who Fought with Custer." The *Halifax Herald*, June 24, 2005.

"Paris Man Survives Custer's Last Stand." The *Paris Star*, July 22, 1976, 3.

Turner, C.F. "Custer and the Canadian Connection." *The Beaver: Magazine of the North*, Hudson's Bay Co., summer 1976, 4.

Willert, James. "The Wedding Ring of Donald McIntosh: DISCOVERED?" Research Review Journal of the Little Big Horn Associates, Vol. 10, No. 2, June 1996.

WEBSITES

Bismarck Dakota Tribune, Tribune Extra. *First Account of the Custer Massacre*, July 6, 1876. *http://genealogytrails.com/main/military/battleoflittlebighorn.html*.

"Donald McIntosh: First Lieutenant, United States Army," Arlington National Cemetery. *www.arlingtoncemetery.net/donaldmc.htm*.

"George Armstrong Custer," *New Perspectives on the West*, PBS. *www.pbs.org/weta/thewest/people/a_c/custer.htm*.

Major Marcus A. Reno, "The Official Record of a Court of Inquiry Convened at Chicago, Illinois, January 13, 1879, by the President of the United States Upon the Request of Major Marcus A. Reno, 7th U.S. Cavalry, to investigate his conduct at the Battle of the Little Big Horn, June 25-26, 1876," University of Wisconsin Digital Collections. *http://digicoll.library.wisc.edu/cgi-bin/History/History-idx?type=turn&entity=History.Reno.p0546&id=History.Reno&isize=M*.

"Mark Kellogg's Last Letter," the *New York Herald*, July 11, 1876. *http://www.astonisher.com/archives/museum/mark_kellogg_big_horn.html*.

Wommack, Linda. *Chief Black Kettle presented by Dancing Eyes*. *www.manataka.org/page161.html*.

OF RELATED INTEREST

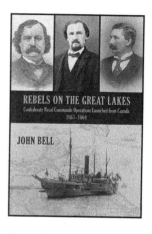

Rebels on the Great Lakes
*Confederate Naval Commando
Operations Launched from Canada,
1863–1864*
By John Bell

978-1554889860
$27.99

Since the terrorist attacks of 9/11, a myth has persisted that the hijackers entered the United States from Canada. This is completely untrue. Nevertheless, there was a time — during the U.S. Civil War — when attacks on America were launched from Canada, but the aggressors were mostly fellow Americans engaged in a secessionist struggle. Among the attacks were three daring naval commando expeditions against a prisoner-of-war camp on Johnson's Island in Lake Erie.

These Confederate operations on the Great Lakes remain largely unknown. However, some of the people involved did make more indelible marks in history, including a future Canadian prime minister, a renowned Victorian war correspondent, a beloved Catholic poet, a notorious presidential assassin, and a son of the abolitionist John Brown.

The improbable events linking these figures constitute a story worth telling and remembering. *Rebels on the Great Lakes* offers the first full account of the Confederate naval operations launched from Canada in 1863–64, describing forgotten military actions that ultimately had an unexpected impact on North America's future.

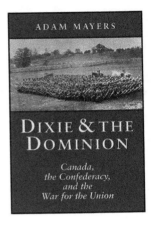